HISTORIC
MAINE
HOMES

300 Years of Great Houses

—HISTORIC—
MAINE
HOMES

300 Years of Great Houses

Photography by **Brian Vanden Brink**   *Text by* **Christopher Glass**

Published by Down East Books
A wholly owned subsidiary of The Rowman & Littlefield Publishing Group, Inc.
4501 Forbes Boulevard, Suite 200, Lanham, Maryland 20706
www.rowman.com

16 Carlisle Street, London W1D 3BT, United Kingdom

Distributed by National Book Network

Design by Linda Chilton

British Library Cataloguing in Publication Information Available

Library of Congress Cataloging-in-Publication Data

The hardback edition of this book was previously catalogued by the Library of Congress as follows:

Vanden Brink, Brian, 1951¬–
    Historic Maine homes : 300 years of great houses / photographs by Brian Vanden Brink ;
  text by Christopher Glass. — 1st ed.
        p. cm.
    Includes bibliographical references and indexes.
    1. Architecture, Domestic—Maine. 2. Historic buildings—Maine. I. Glass, Christopher. II. Title.
    NA7235.M2V26 2009
    728.0974—dc22
                                                            2009024707

ISBN 978-0-89272-799-5 (cloth : alk. paper)
ISBN 978-1-60893-288-7 (pbk. : alk. paper)

∞™ The paper used in this publication meets the minimum requirements of American
National Standard for Information Sciences—Permanence of Paper for Printed Library Materials,
ANSI/NISO Z39.48-1992.

Printed in Malaysia

DEDICATION

This book is dedicated with respect, admiration, and gratitude to the builders of these houses, clients, architects, and craftsmen, without whom they wouldn't have come into being; to the enthusiastic later owners and societies that have kept them from destruction; to all of my friends and colleagues at Maine Preservation and the Maine Historic Preservation Commission over the years, who have worked to ensure the appreciation and safety of the houses; and especially to Earle G. Shettleworth, Jr., the keeper of the flame of Maine's historic architecture. And, as always, to my wife Rosalee.

Note on the Photographs

Brian Vanden Brink's archive of photographs of Maine houses was the inspiration for this book. Though he had most of the important houses, he had missed a few that were needed to tell the whole story. The Maine Historic Preservation Commission (MHPC) generously opened their files, which are an impressive collection of postcards, stereo views, and photographs both early and current. In addition I drew on photographs taken by Elizabeth Bouvé, who had attended one of my lectures and volunteered to make better pictures than the ones I was using. She has since traveled the state fulfilling that promise. I am very grateful to her and to the Commission staff for their help.

Contents

A quiet corner of the Hamilton house.

Preface

Maine is most well known for its natural beauty, its seacoast, lakes, and forests. For those who live here, it is also a place of towns and villages, of farmsteads and houses from all the generations who have come before. Our houses tell the most personal of stories. Each generation built houses to express its beliefs and aspirations. The great houses were built to celebrate their owners' accomplishments, and the more modest houses tried to borrow some of the splendor of those trendsetters. My goal is to tell the stories of our houses (beginning with the very first) as revealed through the stories of particular "great" houses. In brief, the overall story is this:

The earliest buildings of European exploration were designed simply to keep out the weather. Most of these have gone now, though archaeologists have examined clues to early construction in places like Pemaquid and Castine. As fishing and maritime trade grew along the coast, and farms and logging operations spread inland, permanent towns were built, and home owners began to try to incorporate the fashions of the home country. The 18th century was the age of imitating England.

After the Revolution, tentative steps were taken toward a more modest kind of house, better suited to the ideals of a new republic, and to the exigencies of a disrupted economy. Beginning in the 1820s, a continuing wave of new styles proclaimed builders' allegiances to changing ideas of what a house should be. First, the Greek Revival adopted the architecture of ancient Greece—the first democratic republic. The Gothic Revival followed, evoking the romance of the days of chivalry and the church. Then the young Queen Victoria's favorite style, called Italianate, swept the state of Maine. All these stirred together to become the Queen Anne Victorian style, which today is simply called Victorian. A reaction to the excesses of the Victorian style led to the rediscovery of Colonial architecture and its rural offshoot, the Shingle Style. By the end of the 19th century, several styles of architecture were equally available, each for a different purpose.

Of course, none of this is unique to Maine. These fashions spread throughout the country and mirrored developments in England, which, despite independence, had remained the style setter of American fashion. In Maine, the styles all tended to have early adopters and later imitators. The early adopters copied the full style, complete with radical changes in floor plan and construction. The imitators tended to keep the Maine idea of a house—a rectangular box with a door in the middle and two windows on each side.

In the 20th century, foreign styles began to lose their appeal. Our houses tended to follow the more traditional Colonial Revival (or "Colonial" for short) style or the variations of it available from designers and manufacturers of Craftsman or Sears Roebuck cottages. Summer cottages provided an opportunity to play with different styles based on old fishing shacks and logging camps. Today, most year-round houses still follow the lead of the house plan magazines, and many are prefabricated and delivered to the site more or less complete. In many ways the 20th and early 21st were less interesting centuries. The state's economy has been less robust and therefore house building has generally been a more modest enterprise.

One positive aspect of this changing view of house building has been the increasing value we place on older houses, those that tried for something beyond convenience and comfort. The move to restore old houses to their original appearance was an offshoot of the Colonial Revival. Early efforts to restore Mount Vernon and Monticello led to similar efforts throughout the country, and people have come to appreciate the craft and elegance of the early builders. As appreciation grew, so did the idea that a home should be carefully crafted rather than hastily put together, and it should be adapted to its site the way old houses had been, rather than simply deposited with no regard to orientation or landscape.

In this new century we have become aware of the negative aspects of building uniform suburban developments cut off from both village life and from a genuine sense of the natural landscape. New planning has tried to recreate the ties between house and town and to rethink how a house fits its site. Increasing concerns about the cost of energy have led us to rethink our sources of heat and electricity and our dependence on cars, opting for smaller houses closer to town.

This book will follow the history of these developments. Maine's most important houses form the core of the book and I have woven together a story that traces what inspired their owners and builders to design and build them the way they did. I also suggest ways in which we can learn from the houses and learn to love them for what they tried to do.

I have primarily been engaged in the practice of architecture, mostly building and renovating houses, though I have had opportunities to help restore historic houses and to build new additions to historic neighborhoods—additions that try to show respect for the local traditions. I even had an opportunity to help with the perpetuation of the greatest modern house in Maine. I come to this story, then, with a long experience of thinking about why houses are designed and built the way they are. These reasons have changed with the generations, and seeing what they were helps us to discover our own reasons for shaping our houses the way we do. With luck, maybe it will lead us to do it better.

So let us begin at the beginning and follow the story of how we have built our houses. We are surrounded by treasures and, in uncertain times, it is both important and invigorating to draw inspiration and courage from what their builders achieved.

COLONIAL
1600–1720

The insecure nature of the original settlements influenced building to the extent that

many of the earliest buildings were constructed of solid, squared logs so they could serve as defensive retreats during attacks by either native people or competing Europeans. These houses have come to be called "garrisons," though they were not military barracks and were at the time called "log houses"[1]. The overhanging upper floor was long thought to be a means of repelling attackers by pouring hot water or firing rifles through loopholes in the floor, and in fact this was a feature of some of the blockhouse forts along the coast and rivers, but the overhang really derives from the joinery of the wooden frame of the upper floor. Most houses were built with post and beam framing, but few have survived intact. The log houses may have survived simply because they were too difficult to demolish.

Another peculiar building type is the Old York Gaol, long thought to be of 17th century construction, but now believed to date from the 1720s. The stone center was the gaol, or jail, and the house was built around and on top of it— perhaps the earliest example of the home workplace, and this one in rather unusual circumstances.

Elizabeth Bouvé

THE CAPE

But the most common type of house to evolve during the early period was the Cape, or Cape Cod. The name did not appear until the late 19th century, when art historians from Boston defined the style based on the houses they saw during summer jaunts to the Cape. In fact, the form derives from English crofters' cottages now most often found in the extremities of the British Isles. Capes have been built in Maine ever since. They are the fundamental icon of the house: pitched roof, center chimney, and the inevitable façade of door in

Not many buildings survive from the earliest period. York was one of the oldest settled areas, and the Perkins House of 1730 (facing page), the McIntire Garrison of 1707 (above), and the Old York Gaol (top) are the best examples of the earliest houses.

Center Chimney Capes were the most typical small houses. This one, in Sheepscot, is a reconstruction using an early frame and details typical of the early period.

the middle and windows on each side. Four windows is standard, but capes can be sliced into three-quarter, half, and even quarter capes, depending on the number of windows.

The plan of the Cape is based on the most efficient use of a chimney. The center chimney has fireplaces for both front rooms and a kitchen fireplace for the rear. The kitchen is the heart of the house, with doors leading to the front rooms and to rooms at the rear corners, variously serving as storage or "birthing" rooms. A narrow and winding stair is fitted tightly into the space between the front door and the chimney and leads up to two or more rooms under the sloping roof. In more southern climates settlers put chimneys on the ends of the house, but in Maine the center chimney became the norm, though the dominance of the center chimney was challenged by later generations who were tired of the narrow stair.

Generally, New England's early architecture was wood framed and had clapboard siding. A regular hierarchy of exterior cladding materials developed:

From Barrel Staves To Clapboards

Early houses were usually sided with clapboards—and there's a story behind that. John Alden, the shy suitor of Longfellow's popular poem "The Courtship of Miles Standish," was hired onto the *Mayflower* as a cooper, a barrel maker. An unusual requirement in those days, comparable to bottle deposit laws today, was that anyone taking beer barrels on a sea voyage had to bring back material to make more barrels. That material was called clapboards, and originally referred to barrel staves.

At that time some English buildings, particularly in the area of Lincolnshire, where the Pilgrims came from, did use weatherboarding, but it was generally used only for outbuildings or windmills. Most English cottages were walled with some kind of plastered infill—soft brick or wattle-and-daub—but the plaster available to the Plimouth Plantation was made from burnt oyster shells and didn't hold up in the North American winters. It's amusing to imagine the Pilgrims looking at their crumbling plaster and saying, "Well, now what?" and turning to John Alden to borrow some of his clapboards to cover the outsides of their buildings.

Wikipedia

The Plimouth Plantation in Massachusetts recreates the earliest days of New England settlement. The buildings, based on archaeological and historical evidence, represent the colony in its 1627 form.

Cut stone at the top, followed by fieldstone and brick, then flush boarding (horizontal boards with flush joints), then clapboards, shingles, board and batten, followed last by logs. The higher up the list the type of material, the more expensive it was, and therefore the more elegant it was deemed to be.

Many of Maine's earliest surviving houses are clapboarded Capes. In Wells, a cluster of early capes has been identified. In the center of Damariscotta the Chapman-Hall House is one of our earlier house museums. Rockport has its Conway House, preserved as a farm museum.

The Olson House, though much later, captures the feeling of early Maine settlement in its isolation and simplicity. Andrew Wyeth's paintings give a feeling of the kind of rural life that most Mainers experienced.

"I AND MY CHIMNEY"

One person to notice the shift away from the large central chimney was Herman Melville, who wrote a wonderful short story called "I and My Chimney," in which a curmudgeonly Yankee farmer resists his wife's desire to demolish the great central chimney. In contemplating the social dysfunction caused by removing the central chimney he says:

> In those houses which are strictly double houses—that is, where the hall is in the middle—the fireplaces usually are on opposite sides; so that while one member of the household is warming himself at a fire built into a recess of the north wall, say another member, the former's own brother, perhaps, may be holding his feet to the blaze before a hearth in the south wall—the two thus fairly sitting back to back. Is this well? Be it put to any man who has a proper fraternal feeling. Has it not a sort of sulky appearance? But very probably this style of chimney building originated with some architect afflicted with a quarrelsome family.

To the farmer, on the other hand, his chimney generates universal human harmony:

> It need hardly be said, that the walls of my house are entirely free from fireplaces. These all congregate in the middle—in the one grand central chimney, upon all four sides of which are hearths—two tiers of hearths—so that when, in the various chambers, my family and guests are warming themselves of a cold winter's night, just before retiring, then, though at the time they may not be thinking so, all their faces mutually look towards each other, yea, all their feet point to one centre; and, when they go to sleep in their beds, they all sleep round one warm chimney, like so many Iroquois Indians, in the woods, round their one heap of embers.

Despite his cogent arguments, the farmer's wife is unpersuaded, and the story ends in a standoff. In real life the central stairway won out over the chimney, except in the case of the humble cape.

The hearth at the center of the home was more than a
practical necessity. It was a symbolic center.

THE CHIMNEY

The problem with the early houses, especially when they acquired a full second story instead of the simple low bed chambers under the roof, was the conflict between the central chimney and the stair. While having all the fireplaces share one cavernous central chimney was a convenience of construction, the large chimney was not an efficient user of firewood or particularly successful in preventing downdrafts, and the stairway was cramped, narrow, and twisting. So the chimney began to migrate, and one way to trace early houses is to watch the chimney move.

The first alternative, which some of the earliest Massachusetts and many Virginia houses had used, was to have two chimneys, one at each end. That was not typical in Maine, however, because half the heat went outside. Maine's solution was to have two chimneys (though not at the ends of the house) with a stair hall between them. I have been inside a house with two chimneys and

James and Leila Day's house in Castine shows how the chimneys moved to the sides of the central stair.

a stair hall, but, in that house the two chimneys rejoined in the attic, emerging from the roof as one. That chimney arrangement was not common, however, as it was just too complicated to build. In a house with two rooms on each side of the central hall the, chimney moved to the middle of the wall between them, with a fireplace in each of the rooms. This allowed the central hall to have a generous stairwell, and the stair became the central architectural feature of the interior.

ELLS AND SHEDS

Another aspect of our houses began early on and has developed through the centuries. Houses, especially farmhouses, simply could not contain the activities of a family that often used the house as a workplace as well as a living space. In addition to the domestic activities centered in the kitchen, the homestead had to accommodate taking care of the household animals, tending the home garden and even farm fields, and storing the foods and fuels needed for long winters. Barns and sheds were necessary, and an ell off the kitchen was often used for cooking in the summer, when the kitchen fireplace was just too hot and uncomfortable. These additional structures gradually accumulated and often became connected when they reached the barn, though they rarely started out that way.

In his book, *Big House, Little House, Back House, Barn,* Tom Hubka points out that the weather wasn't really the driving force in building these additions. There are numerous examples of sheds being built nearly, but not quite, reaching to the barn. His conclusion is that the need to diversify away from pure farming and to have home industries to provide supplemental income, especially in the off-season, led to the building of many of these connectors. ✿

A classic center–chimney cape in Harpswell shows the additions and extensions that became common as the houses "settled in."

GEORGIAN

1720–1780

As conditions along the coast and up the rivers improved, people with a bit of disposable

wealth began to look for ways to distinguish themselves, in imitation of the Bostonians and their English models. In addition to importing fabrics and silver, they began importing architectural ideas, in the form of builders' manuals.

So Maine farmers and traders wishing to show their sophistication would either buy the books or hire the builders who had them, and for more than a century most of Maine's houses and churches were based on these principles. Many of these houses are still around, and quite a few have been preserved to give us an idea of what they were like.

One prominent survivor from this era is the Captain George Tate House in Stroudwater, built in 1755. Apart from its unusual inset attic, the only touch of architectural elegance on its exterior is the doorway, which features an arched fanlight framed within a classical pediment. Inside, the massive central chimney allows only for a tightly wound stair from the front hall. The principal rooms have elegant paneling in the Palladian style. Though this was an important house for a significant owner—the Royal Navy's agent for the business of shaping and shipping masts of Maine white pine—the exterior of the house is still relatively sober.

Grand houses appear in the 1700s. The Hamilton House in South Berwick (facing page), though not completed till 1788, is one of the best examples. One of the earliest is the Tate House in Stroudwater (above), still sporting the center chimney.

The same cannot be said of the Lady Pepperrell House in York, built just five years later. In it the high Georgian style is in full flower. The modest door-frame of Stroudwater has become a full two-story pediment held up by fluted ionic columns, and the corner boards have become fully articulated quoins—wooden corners carved in the shapes of stones and reproducing the real stones shown in the Palladian pattern books. There is no central chimney, but four separate chimneys allow for a grand central staircase with three different baluster patterns. The pure formal symmetry and correctly proportioned windows show a dedication to the dictates of the style of the day, especially in

The Tate House has the thoroughly worked-out interior woodwork of the Georgian style.

the neighborhood of Boston. At least some of the striking wallpaper is based on original fragments found in the house, so the interiors, though restored, are a good representation of how the house felt when it was new.

Lady Pepperrell was an ardent Tory; and during the Revolution she abandoned her house and retreated to Boston. The house was looted by the revolutionaries, and after the war she was allowed to buy it back. Few changes have been made since, except for the addition of the two side "piazzas," added in 1923. It remained in the family until it was sold in 1930, and in 1942 it was given to the Society for the Preservation of New England Antiquities (now called Historic New England), which operated it as a house museum until cutbacks induced them to sell it, with restrictive covenants, in the 1980s.

The Hamilton House was built after the Revolution, but its style is emphatically pre-Revolutionary. It closely follows the design of the house being built

Lady Pepperrell's house in Kittery follows the English taste for classical detail very closely. Imported Block-printed wallpaper was a popular way of proclaiming status.

The Pepperrell House also has
a wonderful double stair. The more
elaborate is to the front, and nearly as
elaborate is the one in the rear, for the
family—and servants.

The Hamilton House (preceding pages) was sited to be seen from the river, which was the principal approach when it was built. The view down the river (right) was also important. Multiple chimneys (facing page) reach their most extravagant.

at the same time for Governor John Langdon in Portsmouth, New Hampshire. Though its immediate models are the houses of Portsmouth and Salem, it shares with them the formal presence and solid mass of the great planters' houses along the James River in Virginia. This is evidently what its builder intended. Colonel Jonathan Hamilton was a trader in lumber, rum, and molasses, and he built his house on the bank of the Salmon Falls River in South Berwick just as those he traded with had built theirs along the James. Waterways were very important in early America. Obviously the original Europeans came by water, and for many years the sea and rivers were the best links between communities. Roads were nonexistent or difficult to traverse at best. Most of the surviving pre-Revolutionary great houses were connected to the rest of the colonies by water.

So the riverfront of Hamilton House is intended to make a good first impression. It presents a grand, symmetrical front, steep-pitched hip roof, and four separate chimneys on the outside walls that proclaim the victory of convenience over energy efficiency. The proportions and placement of its windows show an educated builder, and the embellishment of the broken pediments on its dormers defines its aspirations to high style. The interior fulfills the expectations of the exterior. Classical detailing, an elegant stairway with an arched window on the landing, and elaborate wallpaper all define the elegance of the high style of the times.

But, like many of the grand houses now on display as museums, it fell on hard times when Jefferson's trade embargo and the War of 1812 disrupted the New England coastal economy. The house was only restored to its current state after novelist Sarah Orne Jewett convinced Emily Tyson of Boston to buy it in the 1890s. Tyson's daughter later bequeathed the house to Historic New England in 1949. There are several examples of the rediscovery of great early houses from the Colonial Revival period. 🐚

The major rooms have arcades that extend the chimney front the width of the room, creating a rich spatial interplay with the windows.

THE SHAKERS

At the same time the Hamilton and other houses were being built, an intentionally different kind of dwelling was planted in Maine by the Community of Shakers, who lived a life of celibate communal labor and worship shaped by the motto "Hands to work and hearts to God." The Shakers established their community at Sabbathday Lake—then called Thompson's Pond—in 1783, built the meeting house in 1793, and the first of the dwelling houses the next year. It was not the only Shaker settlement in Maine, but today the Sabbathday community is the only one still owned and occupied by the surviving Shakers.

Architecturally, the houses used the common language of clapboard siding and carefully placed and proportioned doublehung windows, but they left off any superfluous decoration. They are the architectural expression of the famous hymn "Simple Gifts," composed by Elder Joseph Brackett of the Gorham community. Its first stanza is a call not just to a way of life, but a way of thinking about buildings:

> 'Tis the gift to be simple, 'tis the gift to be free,
> 'Tis the gift to come down where you ought to be,
> And when we find ourselves in the place just right,
> It will be in the valley of love and delight.

Today the community's lands and buildings have been placed in conservation and preservation trusts, with Maine Preservation holding the preservation easement, so this alternative approach to living on the land the way "you ought to" should be available to visitors for generations to come.

The iron box stove, built-in cabinets, and the peg strip for hanging clothes — and chairs —
are all treated with the careful refinement and attention to spare detail that the Shakers saw
as a form of worship. Their buildings exhibit the same restraint and excellent proportions.

FEDERAL

1780–1830

Historians of our architecture have a political problem. It was easy enough to call the houses

based on English prototypes "colonial," but that word became "politically incorrect" in 1776, when America declared its independence. Any house with a symmetrical front, white clapboards, and doublehung windows is still referred to as a "colonial," since the term was rehabilitated beginning in the 1870s as referring to the houses of our founding fathers. But the houses built after 1776 weren't that much different from the ones built before. Historians distinguish the earlier and later periods by calling the earlier (pre-1776) period the "Georgian," after kings George I – III of England (George IV gets his own period, called the Regency, because architectural fashions had changed by his time), and the later the "Federal," after the new American government.

Unfortunately, there is no clean delineation between styles. Some houses that are called Georgian, like Hamilton House, were built after the Revolution. In Maine not all houses were built to the current most popular fashion. Old ways persisted and innovation was resisted. But what characterizes the Federal style is less dependence on strict models and less classical detail. Federal houses were generally less massive and more delicate—in a word, cheaper, even when they were quite large. This was the age when home-grown American architects emerged to replace the pattern books. Charles Bulfinch in Boston, Samuel McIntire in Salem, Alexander Parris in Portland, Benjamin Latrobe in Philadelphia and later the new city of Washington, and talented amateurs like Thomas Jefferson in Virginia, all adapted European models to the needs of the new republic.

These men experimented with new forms like the rounded bay, and decorative treatments inspired by Roman details discovered in new excavations in Rome. The Adams brothers in England (America was not totally independent after all, it seems) had published a book on these details, and the light and intricate patterns came to relieve the severity of the heavy Georgian

Despite the Revolution, house styles remained pretty much the same for a while. Great mansions like the Nickels-Sortwell House in Wiscasset (facing page) and simpler ones like the Peleg Wadsworth House in Portland (above) continued to be built.

detailing. It was not the last time an archaeological discovery would shape house design in Maine.

Maine experienced a housing bubble in the 1790s and 1800s, built on the success of the shipping trade and development of coastal lands. Many of its great houses were built during this period. The bubble popped with Jefferson's trade embargo with England, and definitively ended with "Mr. Madison's War" of 1812. While it lasted, however, the bubble produced great works. Wiscasset and Castine especially have clusters of these houses and provide townscapes that still retain the feeling of those heady days.

Peleg Wadsworth's house (above) was a sober exercise in dignified design. Nicholas Codd's 1804 Wiscasset house for Joseph T. Wood (facing page) was more adventurous, with its projected center and Corinthian pilasters.

The Longfellow House in Portland owes more to the history of its inhabitants than to any architectural extravagance. We know it as the childhood home of Henry Wadsworth Longfellow, composer of the poems that defined the Revolutionary experience ("Paul Revere's Ride"), the virtues of democratic labor ("The Village Blacksmith"), and the American Indian's place in our common story ("Hiawatha"). He depicted the expulsion of the French settlers from Nova Scotia ("Evangeline"), and even told the story of our inventor of clapboard siding ("The Courtship of Miles Standish"). So it is fitting that he should have grown up in a stolid townhouse built by his grandfather Peleg Wadsworth, a distinguished veteran of the Revolution.

Peleg Wadsworth moved to Portland in 1785, as it was still rebuilding from the British attack of ten years before. He built his house next to his store, turning from patriot to shopkeeper. He was successful, bought land, entered politics, and ultimately moved to a grander house on his land in what is now Hiram, leaving the Portland house to his daughters. It was there in 1808 that Henry came as a child. Following a kitchen fire in 1814, his mother Zilpah added an ell and a third floor, eliminating the original two-sided gable roof in favor of the low-pitched 4-sided hip roof preferred by the Federal style. The windows were changed from small twelve-over-twelve-paned sash to six-over-six panes.

In 1901 the house began its life as a museum maintained by the Maine Historical Society, thus becoming one of the first house museums in the state. It has since experienced the evolution of interpretation and restoration that is the life of such houses. New generations have different ideas of how to best restore and present a historic house to the public. It is appropriate that it should be Henry Wadsworth Longfellow's house, since the goal of his work was to seek new ways of keeping the stories of history alive for following generations.

A house that shows the transition from orthodox Georgian to a new era of more adventurous forms is Montpelier, the mansion General Henry Knox built in 1794 on the St. George River in what is now Thomaston. Knox was George Washington's Secretary of War, and he became what we would call a developer, buying acreage along the sparsely settled coast and inviting, among others, German immigrants to settle the frontier. His house was clearly intended to be a showplace, a statement of the promise of his new venture. Its principal feature is the large oval drawing room that swells the front of the house into a grand bowed extension. This unusual feature is very similar to the house Boston's great architect Charles Bulfinch designed for Joseph Barrell in Charlestown two years before. Whether Bulfinch was directly involved in Montpelier, or gave the idea to Knox's Boston builders Ebenezer Dunton and Tileston Cushing, is not known, but the oval room gives the house a vitality that rigorously rectangular plans never had before.

The other dramatic feature of the house is its double flying staircase lit from above by a roof monitor, which also accesses a walkway with a view down the river. The house is unusual among Maine houses because its principal rooms are on the second floor, in the manner of English and some southern houses. This idea originated with some Italian houses, where the *piano nobile* was above a ground floor that was used by servants. In Maine this has been seen in some Castine houses, but it was uncommon after the Revolution because it was considered undemocratic. Altogether, Montpelier was a grand architectural gesture befitting one of the principal actors in the Revolution.

As with the Hamilton House, though, Montpelier's later history was not happy. The area did develop, but Knox's family did not prosper. A later form of development—the railroad—led to the demolition of the house in 1871. Only one of the outbuildings remain. It now serves as the Thomaston Historical Society's museum. But, also as with Hamilton, the increased interest in the houses of our founders led to a desire to recreate the house. The Knox County chapter of the Daughters of the American Revolution publicly took up the cause, and when magazine publisher and Portland native Cyrus H. K. Curtis showed interest in the idea, a replica of the house was built, not on the original site, where the railway still runs and a boatbuilding plant is located, but on a nearby site where it is prominently placed to be seen not from the river, but from northbound U.S. Route 1 as it exits Thomaston. Every effort was made to rebuild it as it had been, though no detailed plans had survived.

The replica was built in 1929, but funds for its maintenance were hard to come by, and in 1965 the DAR gave the house to the state. The state parks department, however, had to balance the interests of this one historic house against the needs of the whole parks system, and the house continued to have maintenance problems, some caused, ironically, by Curtis's insistence on a fireproof

General Henry Knox built Montpelier in 1794 as the centerpiece of the land he was settling in Waldoboro. Its raised first floor and curved front (facing page) were dramatic evidence of the importance of the house. Its central light well and rich interiors confirmed the impression.

Montpelier's grand gesture is the oval room (above). The house is contemporary with the White House, and the resemblance may not be accidental. In the central well a dramatic flying stairwell leads up to the light (facing page).

replica with hidden masonry walls that wicked moisture up from the clay it was built on. Finally, the Friends of Montpelier were able to acquire the house from the state, and it is currently in good shape with a very active support group.

In our generation it has been hard to generate enthusiasm for preserving existing buildings unless they can be "re-purposed" for a new, profitable role. The idea that we should undertake the rebuilding of a lost monument—Portland's Union Station, perhaps—is beyond the limit of credibility. The people of Thomaston who chose to recreate this magnificent structure, and those who work today to ensure that it not only survives but also becomes the focus for a wide variety of educational and community activities, deserve our admiration and gratitude.

Ebenezer Alden built his own house (facing page) upriver in Union after finishing Montpelier. It is a much more modest, but finely crafted and well-pro-portioned country house. The attic stair (below) is particularly imaginative.

One of the housewrights Henry Knox brought with him to Thomaston was Ebenezer Alden—a direct descendant of John Alden, the clapboard maker. After Montpelier was finished, he went up the St. George River to the beautiful valley where the village of Union now sits. Rather than speculate in land values as Knox had done, he settled in to farming and building houses in the late 18th century. His house is a solid piece of work, much more conservative in its plan than the grand Montpelier, but built for the long haul of raising a family and running a successful farm and store. Its fine interior woodwork is based on the newest pattern books of the time, especially those of William Pain, who made the Adam style available to Maine's builders. It is an unfortunate footnote that General Knox is said to have died from swallowing a chicken bone at a dinner at Alden's house.

The house still sits in its farmstead east of the village center. It has been fortunate in its succession of owners, In the 1960s it was bought and restored by Joe and Hazel Marcus, and today Dave and Suzy Schaub keep it in order. Houses like this can be found throughout Maine, not all with a story of direct descent from the Plimouth Plantation, but still with the solid and careful construction of our craftsmen.

Alden's dining room (above) continues the theme. In Portland, the McLellan–Sweat House of 1801 (facing page) exemplifies the large city houses that were consolidating the new republic in the new century.

After the turn of the nineteenth century, the number of new, elegant houses increased. In Portland a principle architect was Alexander Parris of Boston, who lived in Portland from 1801 to 1812, and though most of his houses are gone today, they set the pattern that was followed in houses that do survive. Perhaps the most notable is the McLellan–Sweat House of 1801. It was long thought to have been by Parris, but is now attributed to local builder John Kimball, Sr. It is the archetypal Federal mansion, with a grand central hall, a double-return stair, and a Palladian window on the second-floor landing. The proportions of its window openings are a perfect example of keeping unity within diminishing sizes as the windows ascend, although the perfection of this progression is actually the result of an alteration by a later owner. In 1828 Charles Q. Clapp lived in the house and decided to "modernize" it by lengthening the first-floor windows. As it stands now, the first floor has long windows, with nine-over-nine paned sash. The second floor has the "correct" six-over-six panes, and the short, third floor has six-over-three to keep the pane sizes uniform while allowing a shorter window for the upper floor. In houses today we are likely to see the number of panes kept the same while the proportion of the panes is stretched or squashed to fit the space. Builders trained in the pattern books and apprentice systems of the times knew better.

The village of Damariscotta Mills has an example of the work of another new and notable builder of the time, Nicholas Codd. There is a tale that he was kidnapped from Ireland by James Kavanagh, but stayed and built houses in Damariscotta, Newcastle, and Wiscasset. The Kavanagh house of 1803 is certainly correctly proportioned and well detailed, and the octagonal cupola is an early version of what would become a more common feature in later styles. It is interesting that the octagon is not set square to the house, but has its corners aligned with the façades. This actually makes the intersections with the roof neater, but it does look somewhat out of order.

In Damariscotta Mills, Nicholas Codd built the Kavanagh House in the new, lighter style. Lower roofs and cupolas were typical elements, as was the central Palladian window.

Samuel Melcher III of Brunswick was another major builder who constructed the early dormitories of Bowdoin College and numerous houses, including one for Bowdoin professor Parker Cleaveland that still stands. Cleaveland, lured from Harvard to the Maine woods, was Bowdoin's first professor of mathematics and natural history, and a major contributor to the young sciences. His house was not ostentatious, but it was solid and correct, appropriate for an educated man of the enlightenment. It retains its extensive ell and carriage house and presents a good picture of what Brunswick looked like in the early years of Bowdoin. In 1992 the college bought it to serve as the president's residence.

In Brunswick, Bowdoin professor Parker Cleaveland hired Samuel Melcher III for his house (this page and following) near the college. It is now the Bowdoin president's residence.

Much grander and more ambitious is the pride of Wiscasset, the Nickels-Sortwell House. It represents the epitome of the Federal style. The elegant three-story facade is a virtual encyclopedia of Federal motifs—not considering the portico, which is a reconstruction from 1915. The ground floor has an arcade like those favored by the Adams brothers and by Benjamin Latrobe, architect of the U.S. Capitol. The door has a fanlight, a persistent carryover from the pre-Revolutionary period, that has been elaborated and enlarged. This one is based on a plate from Asher Benjamin's pattern book. The second and third floors repeat the windows of the first floor, and they are now framed by giant order columns like those on Montpelier, though here they are flattened into narrow pilasters. In the center of the second floor is an elaborately detailed Palladian window, while on the third floor the central window is a lunette, or half-round window, similar to the one in the living quarters of the White House a few years earlier. The central stair hall is open all the way to the third-floor ceiling, where a shallow dome supports a central skylight.

Nickels-Sortwell House in Wiscasset (facing page and above, also p. 36), built from 1807 to 1812, has it all — arcaded ground floor, two-story columns, fanlight, Palladian and lunette windows, and a stairwell with a skylit dome.

The fanlight (above) is much larger than those found on Georgian houses. The sidelight tracery is echoed in the Palladian window above (facing page). The later sunporch (right) extends the drama of the house into the narrow side yard.

The house is a confident statement of prosperity and generosity of scale. Unfortunately, Captain William Nickels timed his extravagance badly. Jefferson's maritime embargo hurt his shipping trade, and the War of 1812 finished it. He died in 1815, and the house was auctioned off in 1818. There seems to be a pattern in all this, the grander the house, the more likely the owner was to fail—at least we still have the houses. The Nickels House went through several owners, serving as a hotel and inn, and was finally bought in 1899 by Alvin Sortwell of Cambridge, whose mother was from Wiscasset. Sortwell restored the house to its place at the center of Wiscasset society, and his daughter became the kind of benefactor every town needs. She bequeathed the house to Historic New England, which still maintains it as one of its principal Maine house museums. Though Captain Nickels had little time to enjoy his grand mansion, the people of Maine have benefited from his ambition.

The modest one-room-deep house Dr. Moses Mason built in remote Bethel in 1813 was enlivened by the murals of Rufus Porter. Fine homebuilding was not limited to the coast.

Another view (below) of the Porter murals shows how they contrast with the simplicity of the rooms. The Rev. Jonathan Fisher's self-designed and self-built house in Blue Hill (facing page) shows his independent spirit in its functionally distributed windows.

Not all the growth was happening along the coast in those days. The rivers led to prime timber and farming country deep inland. One house that shows the penetration of architectural thought into the wilds of northwestern Maine is the Dr. Moses Mason House in Bethel. Simple by the standards of other houses of the time, it was nonetheless a pacesetter for its town. Records show the 1813 house was the first in Bethel to be painted white and set on a raised granite foundation. Moses Mason was a physician, but also one of the town's leading citizens. He served two terms in the U.S. Congress in the 1830s. His house has been carefully restored to the period of his life.

The house is also notable for the wall paintings in the stair hall done in the 1830s by traveling muralist Rufus Porter. Porter provided this alternative to the elaborate imported pictorial wallpapers of the kind seen in the Lady Pepperrell and Hamilton houses, and this house has a complete set. Trees appear to grow out of the newel posts, and the experience of climbing the stair is like a panoramic journey along the coast of Maine.

Fisher's no-nonsense interior trim recalls 17th-century work and Shaker simplicity, and looks forward to the arts and crafts sensibility of the early 20th century. This house transcends history.

The Rufus Porter Museum in Bridgton features murals he did in 1828. Porter was a polymath, interested, like Leonardo, not only in painting, but also in invention and science. He founded the magazine *Scientific American,* and in Dr. Mason he undoubtedly found a sympathetic client.

A similarly gifted individual, Jonathan Fisher, also built a house around this time. A Harvard-trained Congregational minister, in 1796 Fisher was called to be the first "settled" pastor in Blue Hill. He was a serious student of divinity and classical languages, and was interested in the sciences and fine arts. His painting of the town from the nearby hill is one of the first landscape paintings we have of Maine.

When he arrived in 1796, Fisher built himself a small cape, assisted by his family and townspeople, who helped raise the house frame. By 1814 the house was too small, so he designed and built an addition. This time he allowed the functional needs to dictate the design of the house and, in so doing, created one of the most idiosyncratic structures in Maine.

Vaguely symmetrical on the main front, the house follows no strict rules anywhere else, inside or out. The plain wood of the interior defies the refinements of the Federal period, recalling earlier, more direct construction methods. The apparently random arrangement of windows, dictated by internal functions, are an architectural repudiation of the strictness of the classical canon. No building of this period better illustrates the architectural principle enunciated by Henry Thoreau in *Walden:*

> What of architectural beauty I now see, I know has gradually grown from within outward, out of the necessities and character of the indweller, who is the only builder—out of some unconscious truthfulness, and nobleness, without ever a thought for the appearance and whatever additional beauty of this kind is destined to be produced will be preceded by a like unconscious beauty of life. The most interesting dwellings in this country . . . are the most unpretending, log huts and cottages . . .; it is the life of the inhabitants whose shells they are, and not any peculiarity in these surfaces merely, which makes them picturesque.

Fisher himself was a man of strong opinions. He was a founding member and strong advocate of Bangor Theological Seminary. "I am strongly adverse to an unlearned ministry," Fisher stated, "but if in this district we wait to be supplied from other institutions . . . the ground would be preoccupied by Sectarians, many of whom will not only be unlearned, but very unlearned." For him religion was best expressed through an active life informed by the resources of cultural and intellectual life. His house is a vigorous expression of that ideal.

The pride of Columbia Falls, the Ruggles House of 1827 is a masterpiece of elegant details and light-filled rooms. It is a condensed version of the grander Federal houses, putting all their elegance into a small gift box.

Even farther Down East, in Columbia Falls, Judge Thomas Ruggles had a house built that is in some ways the opposite of the Nickels-Sortwell House. It is a modest two-story house only one room deep (like Moses Mason's), but within that small compass the builder, Aaron Sherman, packed in as much sophisticated design and detail as he could. The result is an exquisite gem of a house.

The plan is very straightforward—a parlor and dining room with a central stair hall between them. The stair hall is nearly as big as the rooms, and has a double return to the upper floor, which has two bedrooms. There was an ell, which served as a kitchen, but it's not clear whether it was actually part of the original house. There is evidence the cooking was done in the cellar, as was often the case in houses with servants. The ell was removed in the 1930s.

What makes the house distinctive is the attention the builder gave to every detail. He did not simply follow the pattern books and imported Roman motifs. He explored the possibilities of every exterior and interior feature with a lively imagination and sure eye that make this small house in a remote corner of the state one of Maine's true treasures.

Outside, the entry door has a double fanlight under a portico whose openwork cornice is a fantasia of shapes resembling railroad spikes. Who knows where this idea came from. Above the portico is the expected Palladian window, but this one has an extra dip in the muntin, providing an unexpected departure from convention. The stair is astonishing for such a small house, and the two rooms have chimney breasts with contrasting varnished and painted elements that far exceed expectations.

The story of the house is a familiar one. After Judge Ruggles' death, his son Frederick squandered the family fortune. Frederick's daughters kept the house after his death by selling off the family possessions and with the help of the neighbors. After the last daughter's death in 1920, a great-granddaughter, Mary Ruggles Chandler, who owned the pharmacy next door, began the effort to save the house by forming the Ruggles Historical Society and persuading the heirs to donate the house to the society. Since then the society has enlisted friends from all around the region, especially the Bar Harbor community, and their efforts have led to a stable and thriving organization. In 2005 the ell was reconstructed, and the project received an award from the Maine Historic Preservation Commission. Today the tiny Ruggles House preserves the spirit of bringing the elegance and imagination of civilization to the edge of the wilderness.

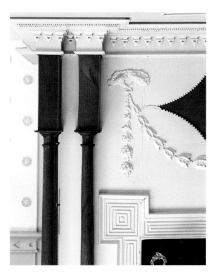

The elegance continues on the exterior, with a fine Palladian window and a porch with non-canonical capitals and an open frieze that seems to anticipate the invention of the railroad spike (above).

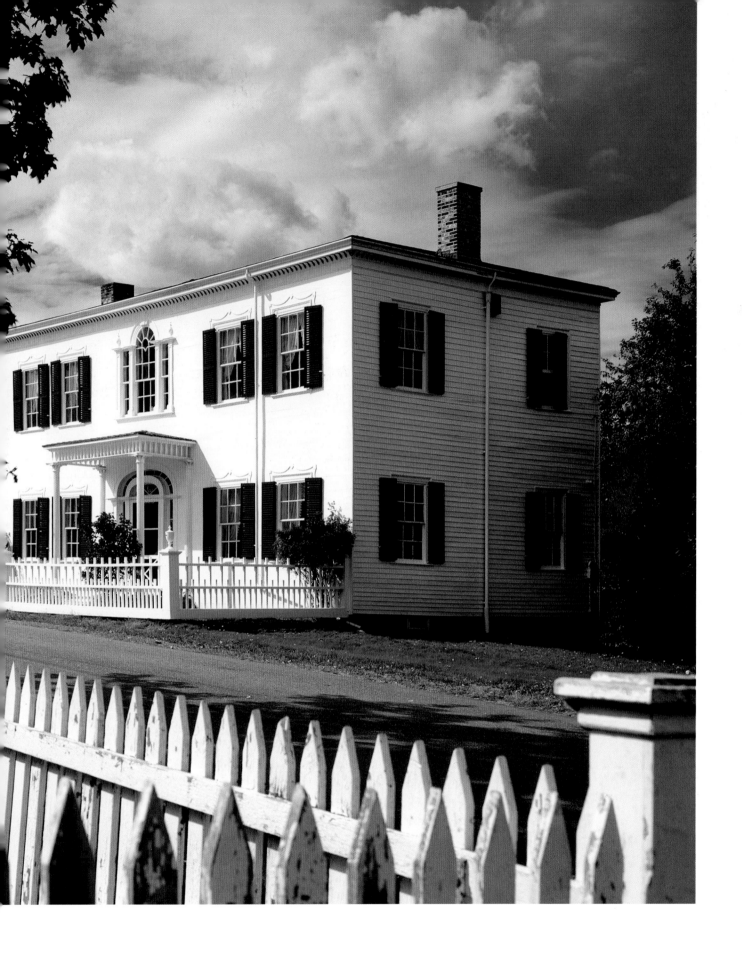

Colonel John Black's unusual house near Ellsworth has no front door. The door in the ell (above) is the main entrance, and the fanlight is reserved for the interior.

Federal houses continued to be built even after new ideas began emerging in the 1820s. One well-preserved example is the Colonel John Black House just outside Ellsworth. By this time fortunes were being made in developing the interior, rather than in trading along the coasts, and Colonel Black was the land agent for the vast holdings bought by Philadelphia developer William Bingham. Not begun until 1824 and not livable until 1828, the house was based on a drawing from one of Asher Benjamin's influential handbooks. The plan did not call for a central hall, but had the main entrance in one of the wings, with two parlors occupying the south front. The name Colonel Black gave to the house, "Woodlawn," may suggest his thinking behind the plan. The house sits on top of a small hill, with an extensive lawn sloping away to the south. Interrupting the connection between the main living spaces and the lawn may have seemed a poor trade for observing the convention of a main front entrance,

The Black House reserves its south front for the large windows of the principal rooms. A gently curving stairwell (facing page) is the focus of the long inner hall.

but the side entrance does allow business visitors to go directly into the office (called the library on Benjamin's plan) without entering the living areas of the house. Perhaps it even foreshadows the almost universal Maine custom of rarely using the front door, entering instead through the kitchen. While the most elegant interior feature—the open curving stair—came from Benjamin's book, his plan did not show the porch across the front. The porch may be an example reflecting a new approach of using classical elements to give dignity to a new house. It also may have been an additional response to the desire to connect the living space with the lawn, or it could conceivably have resulted from the discovery that the south-facing rooms were too warm in the summer. It would be interesting to know when and why the decision to add the porch was made. ✿

GREEK REVIVAL

1820-1850

*U*nlike the change from Colonial to Federal, the change that occurred in the 1820s

represented a revolutionary break with previous ideas about what houses were supposed to look like. As relations with England continued to be difficult, and as new architectural ideas also moved from German and English sources into the former colonies, Americans began to question their allegiance to the inherited forms of English architecture. Further archaeological explorations had led to the publication of the immensely influential *Antiquities of Athens* by British architects James "Athenian" Stuart and Nicholas Revett, and arguments raged over the merits of the Palladian and Greek styles. The Greek style was proclaimed to be more elegant, refined, and purer, since it was based on the style from which the Romans had derived their gaudier, more pompous imitations. Stuart created some buildings based on the Greek orders, and John Nash built the ranges along George IV's Regent's Park in the style, but the architect most enthusiastic for Greek style was Karl Friedrich Schinkel of Germany. In 1818 William Strickland designed the Second Bank of the United States as a Greek temple. Other public buildings followed throughout the country.

And at this point, in 1820, the Greeks went to war to overthrow their Turkish rulers. Americans hailed their efforts as analogous to our own revolution. Many, such as Thomas Jefferson, had likewise hailed the French Revolution, but its excesses had dimmed American enthusiasm. Now, little Greece had dared to rise against the Ottoman Empire, and the analogy to the American Revolution was much better, primarily due to the fact that Athens was the cradle of democracy—however limited that democracy had actually been (women and slaves need not apply, as was also true of our revolution). What had been an intellectual preference for the purity of the Greek style now became an expression of patriotic solidarity.

The Greek style appears in the strict Doric of the Nathaniel Hatch House in Bangor (1832, above) and in the complex composition of Calvin Ryder's White House (left) in Belfast.

Greek Revival

The Greek revolution was the war Lord Byron covered as a correspondent, and Eugene Delacroix had captured the sensationalism of the war with his 1826 painting *Greece Expiring on the Ruins of Missolonghi.*[1] William Cullen Bryant, the influential New York poet and editor, expressed the national mood in an 1823 speech:

> Nothing ignoble or worthless can spring from so generous a stock. It was in Greece that civilization had its origin. It was there that poetry, sculpture, all the great arts of life, were invented or perfected, and first delivered down to succeeding generations. Greece was the real cradle of liberty in which the earliest republics were rocked. We are the pupils of her great men, in all the principles of science, of morals, and of good government.[2]

And of architecture, too. The pattern books began to show how to adapt Greek style for churches and houses. Asher Benjamin, long the standard setter for correct house design, published an amended edition of his *American Builder's Companion* with Greek plates in 1827.

Delacroix's inflammatory painting was part of the wave of enthusiasm for all things Greek that led to such masterpieces as the White House's temple-entry pavilion and cupola.

Charles Q. Clapp's Portland house of 1832 had a full temple front, with a real entry porch and a matching false entry porch. Turning the gable end toward the street was the real "revolution."

Houses that had always had the ridgeline of the their roofs running parallel to the front elevations were rejected in favor of "temple front" houses with the roof ridge at right angles to the front elevation—a literal "revolution"of ninety degrees—so what had been the side wall became the front, with the temple formed by the pitched roof of the gable. There were attempts to introduce a full, freestanding colonnade across the front as Strickland had done in Philadelphia, and houses like the Nathaniel Hatch House in Bangor strove to be totally accurate replicas of the Parthenon. The Hatch house, built in 1832 using designs by Bangor's brilliant Charles G. Bryant, had a full Doric order with colonnaded porches at each end. The Greeks called this the "amphiprostyle"—one benefit of Greek architecture is that you get to use lots of wonderfully impenetrable terms. The Hatch house even incorporates a correct acroterion in the tympanum of the pediment (see what fun it is?). In Greece the acroterion (a decorative motif) would have been placed on the roof ridge, but Bryant knew too much about winter in Maine and instead applied the motif to the pediment, that part of a house's face that is above the horizontal block of the building.

MHPC

In Portland the difference between the old and the new ways of designing houses is shown dramatically in a comparison of the McLellan-Sweat House of 1801 and the Charles Q. Clapp House of 1832. The older house is a fine example of Palladian classicism: carefully proportioned, diminishing windows, a very low-pitch roof surrounded by a balustrade, and, of course, a Palladian window above the door.

Charles Clapp had lived there and lengthened the first-floor windows in 1828, but by 1832 he decided to try the new style. His new house next door, which he seems to have designed himself, violates all of the old rules, even to the extent that it is difficult to determine just where the front door actually is. His house is semiperipteral, meaning the columns go half way around the exterior. On one side is the front door, on the other a window into a storeroom, but the two porches demanded by the style are identical, even to the flights of steps leading to the porch with no door.

The Clapp House is an extreme example. More common are houses that retain the familiar basic forms of the cape or the two-story Palladian block and simply change the decorative detail. That is the pattern for Maine houses over the rest of the century—each time a new style erupted, enthusiasts adopted it entirely, and then the visual elements of the new style were applied to the conventional house plan. By 1842 the term Greek Revival had been introduced in England. Usually when a term is introduced that defines a style, its influence has begun to wane, and it is seen as a separate and passing phase of history. Until that time, it is the "modern" style, whatever its characteristics may be.

Clapp had lived next door in McLellan-Sweat (see p. 46). His new house declared the Federal period to be at an end. Note the extra shutters on the lengthened ground-floor windows.

Rockland's Snow House of 1861 (above) shows the style used on a conventional plan. The temple front has to be achieved by adding a small roof for the central bay. On the interior, the conventional plan allows for a stair hall not too different from the Federal style, in the White house (facing page) as well as the Snow House.

The Snow House in Rockland, probably not built until 1861, was based on a plate from Edward Shaw's handbook and has the characteristics of the mature Greek Revival applied to a conventional plan. Wide but shallow plain pilasters define an engaged colonnade across the front, and the central element, which in McLellan-Sweat and similar houses was a Palladian window above a fan-lit doorway, is now a miniature Greek portico, complete with the acroterion motif in the pediment. The door has a shallow porch supported by four correctly proportioned Doric columns. Clapboards have been supplanted by flush boards intended to make the house look made of masonry rather than wood.

A more conventional example is the 1854 Farnsworth Homestead in Rockland, open to the public as part of the Farnsworth Art Museum. The pilasters have been moved out to the corners of the building, and the entrance is essentially just a door frame, but with pilasters and cornice that repeat the house trim on a smaller scale.

The most thoroughly thought-out example of this approach to the style is the White House in Belfast, designed in 1840 by Calvin Ryder. Ryder was a local architect, originally based in Frankfort, who built houses and other buildings from Camden to Bangor. He eventually moved to Boston and adopted newer fashions from France in place of the Greek Revival.

Interior trim and fireplace details carry the Greek theme throughout the White House. The corner blocks of the door frames are carved in the acroterion motif.

The White House is theatrically sited at a fork in the road as it enters Belfast from the south. Its dramatic two-story temple portico successfully draws attention away from the fact that it is not a temple-fronted Greek Revival, but a Federal house in Greek dress. The cornice of the cupola is loosely based on one of the principal touchstones of Stuart and Revett's *The Antiquities of Athens*: the Tower of the Winds in the Athens agora. Otherwise it is not that different from the cupolas on Federal houses such as Nicholas Codd's Kavanagh House of 1803.

Although these Federal blocks with Greek accents essentially abandoned the revolutionary aspect of the temple-front house, the smaller temple-front plan did survive. A good example is the 1858 A. W. West House on the green in Bethel. The only remaining features of the colonnade across the front are the two corner pilasters and the continuous cornice across the front. This cornice would soon be eliminated as impractical, leaving only the "return" of the eave to recall the original full cornice. The house plan had to solve the problem of the narrow street front, and the solution was a door not in the center but to one side, allowing the rooms to take up two thirds of the width of the house. This plan had been used for row or town houses, first in England and then in American cities, but such houses were rare in Maine outside of Portland. The "half Cape" was also a forerunner of this plan, but it was regarded as a not quite respectable variant of the real cape, which had a symmetrical façade.

Small temple-front houses became popular partly because they could be built on smaller town lots, and in them the two major rooms could be opened up into a double parlor, rather than being separated by either the old central chimney or the newer central stair hall. Because this style was practical, it persisted for a long time after other house styles became fashionable. Just as basic Capes would continue to be built, so would temple fronts, so now there were two fundamental house plans in Maine.

The extent to which the Greek Revival penetrated architectural thinking in Maine is indicated by the presence of three tiny houses in remote North Anson. Probably built as worker housing by a local mill owner, these houses originally had just Greek-detailed front faces, but those are now extended into front porches and perfectly express the goal of the style—to celebrate the connection between the ideals of democratic ancient Greece and modern Maine. 🌸

In Bethel, the West House (top) shows how the style was adapted to less ambitious tastes—the large corner columns and continuous cornice, along with the square-rimmed front entry, refer to the full temple front. Three little temple houses (above) survive in North Anson.

GOTHIC REVIVAL
1840–1860

Elizabeth Bouvé

*T*he Greek Revival had competition nearly from its inception. In 1819 Christ Church in

Gardiner was built in the Gothic style. It was designed by the Rev. Samuel Farmer Jarvis, who was the son of the bishop of Connecticut—where famed architect Ithiel Town had built Trinity Church in New Haven in 1814. The style was derived from the architecture of the middle ages and had an "odor of sanctity" about it. It was not limited to churches, however. English architects as early as Christopher Wren in 1681 and John Vanbrugh in 1719 had used Gothic Revival for university buildings and country houses. Wren used it to complete the unfinished Tom Tower at Christchurch, Oxford, and said it "ought to be Gothick to agree with the Founders worke." Vanbrugh designed himself a castle-like country house to remind himself—and his guests—of his imprisonment in the Bastille as a British spy. Sir Horace Walpole designed himself a Gothic house and published the first Gothic novel, *The Castle of Otranto* in 1764, establishing the fashion for such architectural follies and tales of medieval adventure. Sir Walter Scott's novels followed; he published *Ivanhoe* in 1819, the year the church in Gardiner was built. So Gothic Revival was typically employed to evoke historical associations or more lurid and romantic images.

The first major Gothic house in Maine was in Gardiner, where the first Gothic church was. The Gardiner family house, Oaklands, burned on November 2, 1834, about two weeks after the Houses of Parliament in London burned. The Gardiners decided to rebuild in stone and consulted Richard Upjohn, the English architect who had settled in Boston and was making a name for himself as a designer of Gothic churches. He had been building in the Greek Revival style (he designed the Isaac Farrar House in Bangor in 1833), but had now

Gardiner's Gothic Episcopal Church (above) of 1819 began the Gothic experiment. The style was adopted by less strict house builders to become what is called "carpenter Gothic", like this splendid example, the Shurtleff House in Winslow (facing page).

RESURGENCE OF GOTHIC

Gothic became an official style in England when the Houses of Parliament were rebuilt in the style after the fire of 1834, and in the United States when the Smithsonian Castle was begun in 1847. But it took a visionary to convince the general public to build Gothic cottages to live in. That visionary was Andrew Jackson Downing of New York. Beginning as a nurseryman and landscape designer, he wrote about picturesque landscape design and in 1842 collaborated with architect Alexander Jackson Davis on a book of cottage designs. This major work, published shortly before his early death in 1852, was *The Architecture of Country Houses.* Advocating the country as a better environment for raising a family, he argued that the best house for a working man was a "snug and economical little home in the suburbs" and that the best model for such a home was a cottage based on the medieval English cottage. Along the way he takes on the Greek Revival:

> The temple cottage is an imitation of the Temples of Theseus or Minerva, in thin pine boards, with a wonderfully fine and classical portico of wooden columns in front. The grand portico covers, perhaps, a third of the space and the means consumed by the whole dwelling. It is not of the least utility, because it is too high for shade; nor is it in the least satisfactory, for it is entirely destitute of truthfulness: it is only a caricature of a temple—not a beautiful cottage.

Truthfulness is the quality Downing most admired in a building—truthfulness to site, to station, to materials. Wood imitating stone was untruthful, houses imitating temples were untruthful, and exaggerated architectural gestures were untruthful. Wooden buildings should have vertical board siding. Chimneys should not be disguised, since they are the central feature of a house in a northern climate. And the more nearly a 19th-century American dwelling resembled a 14th-century English cottage, the "truer" it was to the ultimate meaning of architecture.

Maine was not fertile ground for this theory. Conservative carpenters tended to build what they knew, and standard house plans could be adapted to include Greek details. But the Gothic ideas required plans with ells and porches and steep roofs and new kinds of windows and siding. Very few Gothic houses were built in Maine, and those that were often required architects from away to do it.

The Smithsonian's "castle" by John Renwick is the most famous Gothic building. Brunswick's (and Bowdoin's) most impressive Gothic building is the Boody-Johnson house of 1849 (facing page).

adopted the new style. The new home he designed for the Gardiners was a battlemented stone house that Nathaniel Hawthorne called a "castle or palace."

A few other major houses followed. In Portland the John J. Brown House of 1845 was designed by another English architect, Henry Rowe. It featured horizontal boards cut to look like stone, violating Downing's precepts even though the basic plan came from Downing's book. This is the house that became briefly famous when it was moved a mile down Spring Street rather than being demolished when threatened by street widening. Other Gothic Revival houses appear in widely scattered areas. There are a few small cottages that follow Downing's plans, and there are even three examples, two in Waldoboro and one in Brunswick, of an attempt to make a Gothic cottage more picturesque by turning its ell plan 45 degrees and setting the entrance at the joint of the ell. Added to this is an ell at the back, so the house forms the shape of a Y. Evidence that these are Gothic Revival can be seen in the board and batten in Brunswick and the roof trim in Waldoboro.

A Maine house that appears in Downing's book is the Boody-Johnson House in Brunswick, designed in 1849 by yet another English architect, Gervase Wheeler. It is built of wood, with proper vertical boarding and battens. Richard Upjohn, by now the premier Gothic architect of the day, was at work

Richard Upjohn brought stone Gothic back to Gardiner in 1835, after the Gardiner family's house, Oaklands, burned. One of its most dramatic examples is the elaborate remodeling of a Federal house (facing page) in Kennebunk by a sea captain who had seen Milan's cathedral. It is locally known as the "wedding cake" house.

The Architect's Dream

A useful image to explain the Gothic Revival is a painting done in 1840 for Ithiel Towne, the architect of that New Haven, Connecticut, church that inspired the Gardiner church. He commissioned the visionary painter Thomas Cole to create an allegorical painting called *"The Architect's Dream."* In it the architect, perched on a classical column, surveys the vast history of architecture. On one side of a classical harbor the great monuments of Rome, Greece, and Egypt recede into the distance. On the near side of the harbor is a northern forest with a Gothic church. The sun is rising, and its rays penetrate the stained-glass windows of the steeple. The architect, gazing at the church, turns his back on the glories of the past. Clearly, the proper source for inspiration will henceforth be the Gothic, not the classical styles. Towne, by the way, thought the painting was preposterous and refused to pay for it.

*The architect sees that Gothic is the future, and classicism the past,
in this fantasy by Thomas Cole.*

on the Bowdoin Chapel—as well as the First Parish Church and St. John's Episcopal Church in Brunswick. Wheeler claimed experience with Gothic design and briefly worked with Upjohn on the interior of the library section, Banister Hall, of the Bowdoin Chapel. According to Patricia McGraw Anderson, Wheeler was an "unabashed opportunist" whose estimate for the Boody house was half the final cost and who left town owing money. It could be argued that enthusiasm in Maine for the Gothic began to wane at that point.

Curiously, the survival of the style can be seen in summer Bible camps. The camps started as tent meetings, in which individual churches had platforms and made tents available to their members. The tents were gradually replaced with small cottages, often in the morally correct Gothic style. Such

Bible camps like Bayside and Old Orchard Beach evolved from tents on platforms to tiny cottages in the Gothic style. This is a view of Bayside (above).

Elizabeth Bouvé

camps as Bayside, near Belfast, survived and have become year-round communities. With their combination of religious fervor and romantic rustication, these camps perfectly express the ambitions of the Gothic style—to be at the same time both morally uplifting and explicitly out of the ordinary.

The extraordinary remodeling of a house in Kennebunk is another monument to the appeal of the Gothic. The "wedding cake" house, as it is affectionately known, began life as a solid, brick two-story Federal house built by sea captain George Bourne. On a visit to Europe after his retirement, the Milan Cathedral fired his imagination, and he built a carriage house with elements recalled from that inspiration. When that was finished, he decided to make the house more compatible with the carriage house and built an ornamental screen of Gothic detail around the entire house. 🐚

One unusual Gothic design is the Y-shaped house. This surviving example in Brunswick (above) shows how the two branches of the Y face the street. The stem of the Y is the kitchen ell at the back. A new plan for a new age. In 1845 English architect Henry Rowe designed the John J. Brown House in Portland (facing page).

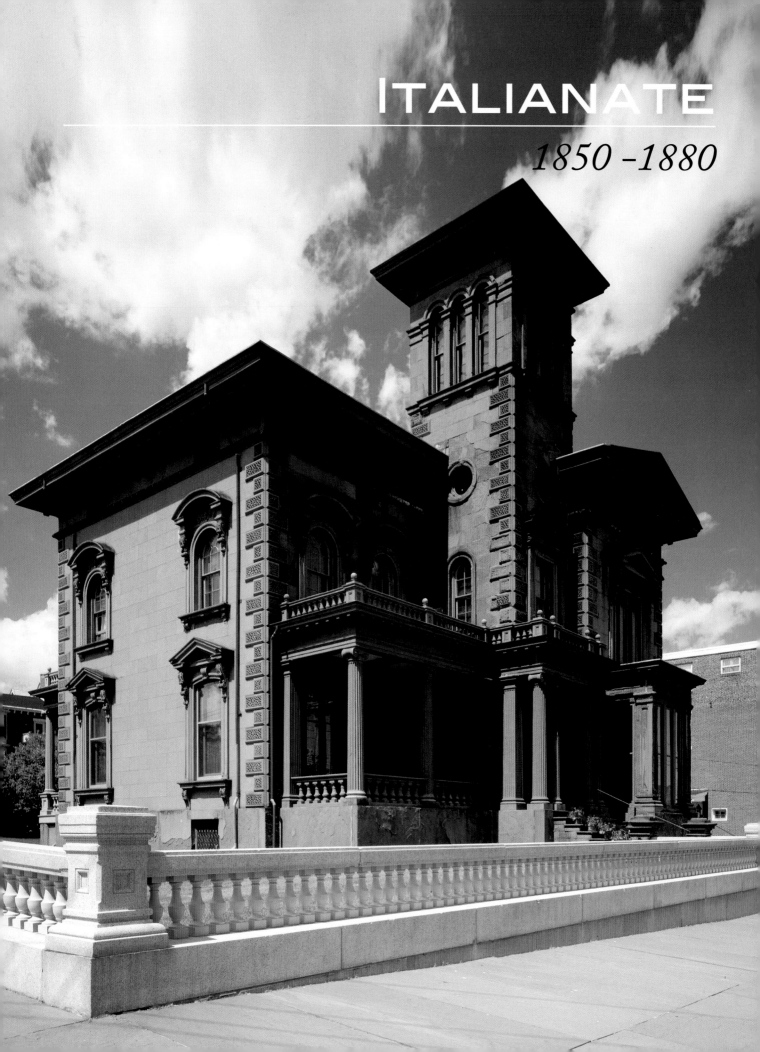

Italianate

1850 –1880

*A*nother wave of architectural enthusiasms soon replaced the passion for things Gothic.

In some ways the new wave was a continuation of the classical traditions of the Federal style and a return to rectangular box-shaped houses, but it was also based on serious architectural philosophy from Germany, primarily in Munich, calling for a return to Roman roots. At the same time this new style acknowledged the romantic appeal of northern Italian adaptations of Roman motifs. The Germans referred to it as Romanesque or *rundbogenstil* ("round-arched style"} because of the return to Roman arches from the obsession with purely Greek elements. In addition to being Roman, the new style allowed greater freedom and more "romantic" shapes of the kind that had appealed to the advocates of Gothic.

None of this would have made much difference in Maine had it not been for two developments in the 1850s. First, Leonard Woods, the president of Bowdoin College, had dinner with the German ambassador in London, who told him about these developments. Woods then commissioned Richard Upjohn to design the new Bowdoin Chapel in this modern style, creating a building that combined Roman and Gothic into a new, universal architecture. Though Upjohn advocated the Gothic style for Episcopal churches, in his own work he was moving toward the Romanesque, and he was willing to use the style for the Bowdoin Chapel not least because he claimed it would be less expensive. So the chapel was begun in 1845, but was not completed for ten years.

The other important style model was the young queen of England. We think of Victoria in her stern old age, but she came to the throne in 1837 at the age of 19 and married her handsome German cousin Albert in 1840. They

Portland's Morse-Libby House (facing page) is the primary example of the style championed by Albert, Queen Victoria's Prince Consort. They remodeled Osborne House (above) on the Isle of Wight as a summer cottage, thus setting the fashion.

bought Osborne House on the Isle of Wight in 1845 and Albert proceeded to remodel it in the new style he had brought from Germany. Acting as his own architect (Thomas Cubitt did the drawings), Albert added a wing with irregular massing, and two of the new square towers. Victoria and Albert were extremely popular and their new styles became firmly in the fashion throughout the English-speaking world—even in Maine.

Houses soon followed. By the 1850s the characteristics of the style were pretty well codified: roofs were low gables or hips with wider overhangs than Maine had seen, supported by sawn wooden brackets. Originally developed to protect the stucco and stone walls of northern Italy from rain, in Maine these overhangs had problems with ice buildup, but they were in fashion, so people used them. Though the houses were most often simple rectangles, the more adventurous adopted an irregular plan not too different from the Gothic cottages advocated by Downing. Occasionally a new house sported the distinctive innovation of the Italianate style, the square tower, or campanile—another feature of the northern Italian villas. The influential critic of all things architectural and otherwise, John Ruskin, was enthusiastic about this style in general and the square tower in particular, which he called "a constant and most important feature in the Italian landscape" and stressed its importance in "drawing together" the irregular masses of house and outbuildings.

The interiors of the Morse-Libby House, completed in 1858, were decorated and furnished by the leading New York designer Gustave Herter. He had Italian craftsmen brought in for the decorative work.

In 1857 Captain Francis Jordan built a house in the style near the Bowdoin campus and it later became the house of the Bowdoin president who succeeded Leonard Woods. Other houses in Brunswick were built in the same style. There were clusters of the new houses in Bath and Searsport, and in Bangor Benjamin Deane built the Pierce-Giddings House in 1851. Other square towers appeared on the Colonel William L. Thompson House in Kennebunk, and in relatively remote Norridgewock the C. F. Douglas House of 1868 has a pure version, with the tower carefully placed in the corner of the ell.

It was in 1858, however, that the high-water mark of the style was achieved, when Maine native Ruggles Sylvester Morse returned from New Orleans to spend summers in Portland and build the showplace we now know as Victoria Mansion, without a doubt the most elaborate work of architecture and decoration in Maine. Even including the recent crop of gigantic mansions along the coast, Victoria Mansion is one of Maine's and America's great houses, not only for its conception and construction, but also for the level of its preservation and current care.

Morse was very successful in the luxury hotel business in New Orleans just before the Civil War, when "cotton was king" and the shipping trade on the Mississippi made New Orleans the major southern port. He used all his resources as a hotel developer to create his new house. He hired architect Henry Austin of New Haven, Connecticut, who had grown up with the classical traditions, indulged in the Gothic style while working for Ithiel Towne, and built one of the most interesting Egyptian Revival structures as the gate to the Oak Street Cemetery. But he had also become one of the masters of the Italianate style by the 1850s, with houses near (now on) the Yale campus. Of these the Norton House of 1849 bears a strong resemblance to the Morse House. After the Morse house he turned to the later forms of Gothic for the rest of his career. He was truly a man of his times, but always a competent professional with a good sense of proportion. It is said that he considered the Morse House his masterpiece.

The house is the quintessential Italianate villa. Though the plan has the same basic center-hall layout as the McLellan House, not far away, the spaces on each side of the stair hall are very different. On the left is one grand parlor, and on the right a succession of rooms leading to the service ell. The parlor is set back to the rear edge of the square tower, while the music room projects beyond the front of the tower, breaking up the rectangular mass favored by generations of Maine builders and creating the irregular mass that Ruskin admired in Italy.

The house is appropriately known as Victoria Mansion, and is a glimpse of a very non-typical Maine household.

The entrance is through the base of the square tower, and the stair hall rises through the height of the house to a stained-glass skylight—somewhat similar to the Nickels-Sortwell House, but on a scale unimagined by the earlier generation. The house is actually not overly large, but every detail is so thoroughly thought out and well executed that the house seems grand rather than merely big.

Morse not only hired an architect. He commissioned the most important furniture maker of his generation to execute the interior. Gustave Herter of New York designed the elaborate interior. Craftsmen from Italy executed the plaster and paint, and Herter's workshops produced the furniture. So, the house was not filled with the usual heterogeneous collection of individual pieces of furniture, but had a completely coordinated interior. All modern conveniences, from indoor plumbing to gas lighting, were incorporated, and the house even had a Turkish smoking room for the men.

It is interesting to speculate on the extent to which the Morses saw an analogy between themselves and Victoria and Albert. Clearly this modest

Each room has a slightly different decorative scheme, allowing Herter to display the full range of his talents.

vacation home was their Osborne House, intended as much to impress the neighbors as to be exciting to live in.

Morse and his wife Olive spent summers in the house until Morse's death in 1893. Olive then sold the house to Joseph Ralph Libby, whose family lived there until 1928, so the house is officially referred to as the Morse-Libby House. In 1940 the house was threatened with demolition, and a local teacher, William H. Holmes, bought it to save it. He named it Victoria Mansion in homage to Queen Victoria when he opened it as a museum. No one knows whether he knew of the architectural connection to Osborne House, but the dedication could not have been more apt.

The last 69 years have seen ongoing restoration efforts. The brownstone exterior and the brown-painted wood trim have all undergone extensive repairs. Furnishings that had not stayed with the house have been returned. Even the stained glass of the skylight, badly damaged in the 1936 hurricane, has been carefully restored. The efforts of the organization that oversees the work have resulted in the mansion being widely recognized as the best surviving example of the Italianate style in the country.

A more modest Italianate house has also survived relatively intact and has been maintained as a completely furnished example of mid-century life. The Skolfield-Whittier House on Park Row in Brunswick is half of a double house completed between 1858 and 1860 by two brothers who were sea captains.

Double houses were surprisingly common in the 19th century. They were built in all of the popular styles and were not limited to the smaller houses we think of today as duplexes, or what the English wonderfully call "semi-detached" houses. There are numerous double Federal houses, and some of the best Greek Revival houses in Bangor are double, such as Charles G.

Bryant's 1833 Kent-Cutting House, with its circular parlors and spiral stairs. And there are double Queen Anne houses. The double house could be built to a large scale, yet with only half the large expense. It is a more efficient use of an urban lot, and with a third of the exterior wall shared with the neighbor, it is more efficient to maintain and heat than a freestanding house. In our current quest for smarter ways of building dwellings, perhaps it's time reconsider the double house.

In the case of Skolfield-Whittier, the houses are completely separate, with side entrances and separate carriage houses. The only shared space is

Another time capsule is the right half of the Skolfield–Whittier double house in Brunswick, built about the same time as Morse–Libby. It was given complete with furnishings to the Pejepscot Historical Society.

the cupola, which has two stairs, one from each attic. One house was sold and eventually became the headquarters of the Pejepscot Historical Society. The other remained in the family, with few changes in furnishings except for updates to kitchen appliances. Skolfield daughter Eugenie, who was educated in England and an ardent supporter of the arts, married Bowdoin graduate Frank Whittier, who became a Bowdoin professor. After he died in 1924 and Eugenie went to live with her daughters, the house was used only occasionally by the family for summer vacations. In 1982, Eugenie's last surviving daughter gave the house, complete with numerous contents—furniture, fixtures, dishes, dolls, and masses of paperwork, including receipts for the appliances—to the historical society. The Pejepscot director at the time, Erik Jorgenson, described the house as a "bug in amber." And so it remains.

Light fixtures, furniture, bric-a-brac, even the contents of the pantry, all predate the house's closure in 1924. The spaces have the high ceilings and large windows of the style, along with decorative moldings not quite as elaborate as Morse-Libby.

Some final glimpses of the treasures of Skolfield-Whittier.

A house that started life as an interesting brick Federal house with possible Irish influences was dramatically altered after its purchase in 1857 by Captain Richard Tucker. A front porch was added that is, if any style, vaguely Italian. It most nearly recalls an orangerie, a south-facing porch used to house potted orange trees during the winter in France and Italy, and less successfully in England. The porch gives the house the expansiveness and generous scale of the

Another great survivor is Castle Tucker of Wiscasset. Like the "Wedding Cake" house, this was a Federal house than received a substantial alteration, in 1857. The circular bays were part of the original, but the two-story sunroom was added.

Inside, Castle Tucker retains much of the furniture from the time of the remodeling.

The interior was reworked at about the same time and has survived as a time capsule of the period thanks to the devotion of Jane Tucker, a descendant who gave up a budding botany career to take care of her parents and then to take care of the house, turning it into a private museum. It is now owned by Historic New England. The dramatic flying stair in the kitchen and the amazing kitchen sink cabinet are alone worth the visit, and the great orangerie shows us what drama passive solar heating can lead to.

Another major example of the Italianate style, though without the square tower, was built on a farm in remote Livermore. On this modest farm grew up the ten children of the Washburn family. Some of them emigrated from Maine and made fortunes and reputations across the country in business, politics,

The special jewels of Castle Tucker's interior are the exuberant sink counter (below) and the even more daring flying stair. Both are simply detailed, with standard beaded boards on the cabinet and simple balusters on the stair, but their design is a celebration of function.

The Norlands, built in 1867 on a hill in Livermore, was the home of the Washburn family. The six brothers and three sisters combined forces to rebuild the old farm where they had grown up, and they did it in the latest Italianate style.

and the military. One founded Gold Medal flour in Wisconsin, another sold his mill in Minnesota to Pillsbury. Two were congressmen, one a general in the army, another a sea captain. Another founded a newspaper in California and invented what became the Remington typewriter.

The children returned often to the family farm to visit their parents and catch up with each other. In 1867 their parents' house burned, so they built a new house in the fashion of the day and called it the Norlands after a Tennyson poem. It is a simple house

in plan, but its bracketed roof and encompassing piazza proclaim its Italianate heritage. It has the high ceilings and generous windows of the style—the Washburn parents likely had some doubts about its practicality. The house was connected through its ell to a substantial barn, which was destroyed by fire in April 2008, along with the adjoining ell, and is undergoing restoration. The family later added a Gothic library modeled on the one in Hallowell. The local church is next door and the one-room schoolhouse is nearby, so the farm is a complex of different building types all related to this prominent family.

In the 1950s the Washburns hired Billie Gammon, a schoolteacher from Nova Scotia by way of a one-room schoolhouse in Piscataquis County, to organize the family archives in the library. Billie was the driving force behind the creation of the Norlands Living History Center. She convinced the scattered Washburn heirs to donate their interest in the farm to the center, which was designated a nonprofit entity in order to receive donations. She organized the

By the standards of the Italianate style, the Norlands was restrained. About the only extravagance was the profusion of ceiling painting, but even this was modest for the time.

first living history sessions with local people, herself included, acting the parts of those who worked the farm and taught in the school. The center has grown to have an active, year-round, live-in program that gives visitors a first experience of what life was like in rural 19th-century America. It is a model for the active integration of a historic house complex into an educational tool and tourist destination. The heritage of the phenomenal Washburn children is carried on by a living monument to their achievements, and their distinctive Italianate house is at the center of it all.

Another house more important for its owner than its architecture is the house Joshua Chamberlain drastically altered in 1871. What makes it interesting is how Chamberlain changed it. In 1859 he was a young, newly married professor at Bowdoin and bought a simple 1820s cape that had been a boarding house for Bowdoin teachers and students. (Henry Wadsworth Longfellow had boarded there.) After his service in the Civil War, General Joshua Chamberlain returned to Maine, where he served four terms as governor, and to Bowdoin, where in 1871 he accepted the post of president. Rather than moving to a grander house more fitting to his new station, Chamberlain had his house moved closer to the campus in 1869, and two years later he had it jacked up and inserted a new first floor under it.

That in itself was not unprecedented—a one-story house could relatively easily have a new first floor built under it without changing the roof or the foundation. But Chamberlain's new first floor was not an imitation of the architecture of the old cape—it had vaguely Gothic entry and porch and definitely Italianate windows and brackets.

MHPC

The new elements made little reference to the old ones, nor were the old ones changed to accommodate the new ones. Even the front door wasn't converted to a window, but was instead provided with a little balcony where the famous hero could conceivably appear to the throng in his front yard. Conservatively keeping the old, yet assertively embracing the new, the house is defiantly itself. It is an architectural self-portrait, and its preservation a fitting tribute to Chamberlain, another of those protean spirits like Jonathan Fisher and Rufus Porter, interested in many aspects of the busy century. 🐚

A last view of the Norlands (facing page). Above, two views of Joshua Chamberlain's Brunswick house, as he bought it (top) and after he had raised it and inserted a first floor (above).

THE OCTAGON

About the time Italianate was becoming the dominant style, the peculiar phenomenon of the octagonal house caused a mild but widespread sensation. It was not a style in the usual sense of proportions and characteristic details, rather it was the inspiration of one man convinced that shape would solve the problem of the house. In many ways Orson Squire Fowler was a forerunner of Buckminster Fuller and other idealists who regarded the conventional house as a hopeless muddle and believed they had a single, simple solution. Fowler's solution was to build the house as an octagon, preferably made of poured concrete. He published *The Octagon House, A Home for All* in 1849, and starting in the 1850s, and trailing off slowly thereafter, several pattern books pushed the concept.

Fowler's basic contention was that the octagon, by more nearly approaching a sphere than a cube, would have less surface and would therefore be more economical to build and more efficient to heat—much as Buckminster Fuller argued about his geodesic dome. Fowler believed the interactions of a family within the octagon would be easier and more communal, in the same way Melville's farmer thought a central chimney made for brotherhood. Several octagons were built in Maine and some are still standing, in Wiscasset, Bath, Farmington, Biddeford, and other places. Fowler's plans often squeezed conventional rooms into the shape, creating awkward corners and odd circulation. The most elegant octagonal plan was devised for Poplar Forest, the retreat Thomas Jefferson built for himself beginning in 1806. Jefferson's house, however, was not widely known and seems to have played no role in Fowler's enthusiasms. More likely his ideas were the result of thinking by analogy to his other obsession, phrenology, the study of how the shape of the skull determines intelligence and character.

Courtesy of the Corporation for Jefferson's Poplar Forest

Mr. Jefferson's Poplar Forest (above) was the secret progenitor of the octagonal houses promoted by Orson Fowler. Captain George Scott's house in Wiscasset (1855, facing page) is a good example of Fowler's ideas.

SECOND EMPIRE

1860–1880

*I*n November of 1861, Queen Victoria's consort, Prince Albert, traveled to Cambridge, where

their son Edward had failed to break off an "unsuitable relationship." On his return to Windsor, Albert developed typhoid fever and died. Victoria went into permanent mourning, gradually becoming the stern figure known for having said, "We are not amused." The fashions associated with her youth disappeared.

During the same period, France was asserting its cultural identity after the chaos of its revolution, the highs and lows of the Napoleonic era, and the uprising of 1830. In 1852, Louis Napoleon III proclaimed the reestablishment of the French Empire and began a period of reconstruction in Paris that included the royal palace and the Louvre. He ordered that the range of buildings be completed in the style of the 17th century, a characteristic of which was the double-sloped roof penetrated by dormers. That type of roof came to be know as "mansard," because it was used in important buildings by Francois Mansart in the 17th century. The part of the Louvre complex with the strictest mansard roof was the Pavillon de Flore of 1595 by Jacques Androuet II du Cer-

PATRICK GIRAUD

ceau. Confusingly for historians, Mansart's grand-nephew, Jules-Hardouin Mansart, did a major addition to the Louvre in the 18th century, but he did not call for a mansard roof.

While work on the Louvre was going on, Louis Napoleon authorized a major overhaul of Paris's city plan under the supervision of Georges-Eugéne Haussmann. His new plan called for massive demolition of crowded areas with narrow streets, replacing them with broad boulevards. Haussman's regulations allowed a tax break for buildings along those boulevards—if they had a mansard roof. He got the result he wished—elegant boulevards lined with mansard-roof blocks, the Paris we sing of today. The city blossomed and became a center of art and culture, a mecca for sophisticated travelers. Paris was now the center of architectural fashion, so houses in the rest of the Europe-inspired world, including Maine, sported the latest French chapeaus.

ELIZABETH BOUVÉ

The Second Empire Style is also called the Mansard Style, after the 17th century French architect who designed the Pavilion de Flore of the Louvre (above). The style is identified by its roof, a French chapeau above an Italianate dress, as in this splendid example from Richmond (facing page).

The Blake House of 1855 in Bangor (above) set the fashion in Bangor. In Lewiston there is an excellent example (facing page) that recalls Edward Hopper's House by the Railroad.

Probably the first Maine house to be built with a mansard roof was the William Augustus Blake House in Bangor, built in 1857–58. It was designed by Calvin Ryder, who also designed the Greek Revival White House in Belfast. He had moved to Boston, where he could keep up with fashions, and he gave the Blake family the latest thing. Below the cornice line the house is essentially Italianate, but the mansard roof was a new idea for Maine.

The pattern books were not far behind. New York architect Calvert Vaux published his treatise on villas and cottages in 1857, and it is a wonderfully mixed collection of Gothic cottages, Italian villas, and the new curved-roof models, about which he says:

ELIZABETH BOUVÉ

"The introduction of circular-headed windows, circular projections, or verandahs, and of curved lines in the design of the roof, and in the details generally, will always have an easy, agreeable effect . . . and curved roofs especially deserve to be introduced more frequently than has hitherto been the practice here."

MHPC

Another transient style is now called the Stick Style. Based partly on Swiss chalet design, it has ornamental woodwork that does not mimic carved stone. This house (above) in South Berwick is one of the best examples. The mansard also appears on a group of tiny houses in Round Pond (facing page), with inset rather than protruding dormers.

The effect may be easy, but the construction and subsequent maintenance were not. Nonetheless, there are quite a few examples of houses whose roofs speak more of Parisian boulevards than Maine blizzards.

Bangor architect George W. Orff built quite a few houses in the Second Empire style, but Bangor was not the only place they cropped up. Along the Kennebec there is a small, charming house in Richmond, and the more impressive Governor Joseph R. Bodwell House in Gardiner, currently undergoing a much-needed restoration. There is a lovely house on the main road in Cherryfield, and a house in Auburn recalls Edward Hopper's iconic painting *House by the Railroad*. In Portland, Frances Peabody preserved a small but charming example. Throughout the state there are many surviving examples of the pursuit of French fashion.

There is one spot in Maine where a cluster of small mansards appeared, both as new buildings and as additions. It is the village of Round Pond. These are interesting in one respect because several have dormers not projecting out from the sloping roof but set into it, almost as if the builder had misread the drawings. This is a bit like the inset windows on the Tate House in Stroudwater.

France's Second Empire style was nudged aside by other styles that copied European models. There was a brief fling with the Stick Style, based on Charles Eastlake's influential book *Hints on Household Taste in Furniture, Upholstery, and Other Details*, published in England in 1868. A forerunner of the Arts and Crafts movement, the Stick Style stressed showing the components of the construction rather than the finished form—a doctrine of "form follows fabrication" rather than "form follows function." The Hutchins House of 1879 in Waldoboro is a good example of the style, as is the 1870 Edward A. Noyes House in Portland.

There was a resurgence of Gothic in a new, more historically accurate and more elaborate form. And there was a fad for German castles that didn't make much of an impression in Maine, though the 1886 romantic stone castle called Norumbega is now a bed and breakfast in Camden, and The Turrets, in 1893–95 in Bar Harbor by Bruce Price, who designed the influential suburb of Tuxedo Park in New York and the great Canadian railroad hotels like the Château Frontenac in Quebec City, is now the centerpiece of the College of the Atlantic campus.

But by this time there was no longer a specific style to capture the public imagination. The ability to produce elaborate ornamentation by machine and to design and build extremely ornate and intricate houses led to an intoxication with intricacy apart from its authorization by any historic precedent. These houses would in time come to be called the "Queen Anne" style. ✿

A grand specimen of the Stick Style is the Hutchins House of 1879 in Waldoboro (facing page). It would not have originally been painted white. The Germanic stone castle appeared, in Camden at Norumbega of 1886 (top) and in Bar Harbor in Bruce Price's The Turrets, designed in 1893 (above).

QUEEN ANNE

1880–1900

The name of this style may have originally had some irony associated with it. The only

British Queen Anne reigned from 1702 to 1714, and the architecture of her reign was somewhere between high Baroque and early Georgian.

Basically, the Queen Anne style was a free-for-all of the kinds of decorative detail that had been used in the various prior styles. The pattern books, more numerous and elaborate than ever, were supplemented by catalogs of ready-made parts—brackets, finials, turned posts, hardware of all kinds. These were no longer carved or forged by hand, but were turned out on steam-powered machines in factories, many of which had their start supplying the Union Army during the Civil War.

One of the most characteristic examples of the Queen Anne Style in Maine is the Auburn house of newspaperman, novelist, occasional poet, and later, pioneer filmmaker, Holman Day. Built on a corner lot in 1892, it has all the earmarks: filigreed porch, elaborate windows and door trim, complicated rooflines, elaborate interior woodwork and hardware, and a signature corner tower. Frank Lloyd Wright, who began his career fighting against this style, especially disliked corner towers. In his *Modern Architecture,* Wright wrote:

> Unless the householder of the period were poor indeed, usually an ingenious corner-tower on his house eventuated into a candle-snuffer dome, a spire, an inverted rutabaga or radish or onion or—what is your favorite vegetable? Always elaborate bay-windows and fancy porches played 'ring around a rosy' on this "imaginative" corner feature.

"Queen Anne" basically means "anything goes," or as Mae West said, "Too much of a good thing can be wonderful." Towers, porches, dormers, all festooned with ornament that did not pretend to be based on history ran riot in the Gilded Age, as in the 1885 Hartley Lord House in Kennebunk (facing page) and Holman Day's 1892 house in Auburn.

*Writer and filmmaker Holman Day
made his Auburn house a showplace full
of delicate woodwork, and announced
it to the world with a characteristic
"candle-snuffer" corner tower.*

ANNE THE QUEEN

Queen Anne gave her approval for the building of Blenheim Palace, John Vanbrugh's monumental house for the Duke of Marlborough, given to him by a grateful England in honor of his defeat of the French at the Battle of Blenheim. Before the mammoth house was completed, Queen Anne had died, and a no longer grateful Parliament ended the subsidy. One of Vanbrugh's political enemies proposed an epitaph for him that included the lines "Lie heavy upon him, Earth, for he / Laid many heavy loads on thee." Heavy, the palace at Blenheim may have been; it was not, however, in the "Queen Anne" style.

Queen Anne does appear in Thackeray's popular 1852 novel *The History of Henry Esmond, Esq., A Colonel in the Service of Her Majesty Queen Anne,* but that is an unlikely source for an architectural connection. It is perhaps more likely that the idea of referring to her came from Gilbert and Sullivan, whose operetta *Patience* premiered in 1881, running 578 performances at the Savoy. In it the cynical poet Bunthorne confesses his strategy for impressing the gullible, and his song contains the lines:

About the only architecture actually associated with Queen Anne was Blenheim Palace, which she approved as a gift to the Duke of Marlborough.

> Be eloquent in praise of the very dull old days
> which have long since passed away,
> And convince 'em, if you can, that the reign of good Queen Anne
> was Culture's palmiest day.

Regardless of where the name originated, it gave rise to the critical phrase, "Queen Anne front, Mary Anne behind," referring to a building that made a good first impression but upon inspection disappointed.

North Berwick, Me. - The D. A. Hurd Residence.

Extravagant houses like the Hurd House of 1870 (and 1887) made their way into postcards as scenic wonders (above). The Hartley Lord House relegated its out-of-fashion French mansard to the carriage house (facing page).

Mr. Wright notwithstanding, it must be admitted that these houses exemplified William Blake's motto "Exuberance is Beauty." Examples of the style appeared throughout Maine. In Skowhegan there is the 1887 Samuel Gould house, and a great example is Hurd Manor in North Berwick, designed in 1870 and enlarged in 1887 by J. Edward Richardson for Daniel and Mary Hurd. The Hartley Lord House of 1885 is a splendidly maintained example on Captain's Row in Kennebunk. Not only the exterior has been preserved, but a good deal of the original interior as well. Lord was originally from Kennebunk and had the house designed by Boston architect George Meacham. A newspaper review of the time described it as "an elegant structure . . . attractive without being 'loud.'" It was bought in 1981 by Robert Beardsley, who made the major repairs required after nearly a century, but kept the house as close to its original condition as he could.

The complicated roofs and multitude of detail in Queen Anne houses meant that maintaining them was an ongoing chore, and though widespread, the style was fairly short-lived. In fact, the popularity of the fashion lasted only about as long as the first paint job. The upkeep, combined with the financial panic of 1893 (started by the bankruptcy of the Philadelphia and Reading Railroad and cascading to bank failures throughout the country) led to a new and

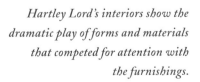

*Hartley Lord's interiors show the
dramatic play of forms and materials
that competed for attention with
the furnishings.*

more restrained approach to house design. The Queen Anne style was the cul-
mination of a century of seeking architectural validation in European fashions.
It gave way to a new attitude in which America looked to its founding fathers
for guidance, and though the founding fathers had also looked to England, that
aspect of their building was ignored. 🐚

SHINGLE STYLE

1890–1910

$\mathcal{T}$*he term "Shingle Style" was not introduced until 1952, coined by Vincent Scully in his*

study of *The Architectural Heritage of Newport, Rhode Island*. Three years later he wrote *The Shingle Style and the Stick Style* (he also introduced that term), and with this book he demonstrated the architectural significance of the houses built with shingled exterior walls around the turn of the century. It is not often that a historian can claim to have "invented" a historical period.

One of the sources Scully cites is a photograph, published in the magazine *American Architect* in 1888, of the 1636 Fairbanks House in Dedham, Massachusetts—believed to be the oldest surviving timber frame-house in North America. The angle of the picture stresses the house's informal plan and integration with its landscape, as Scully describes it:

> Picturesque, powerful in the expression of rough masonry and weathered shingles, it is similar to the best of the original houses of the early 80s themselves. As a colonial house it plays a rich part in a counterpoint of vision and influence into which academic rigidity does not enter. An antiquarian love of colonial things has been transformed by free imagination into an original architectural synthesis.

Here two ideas are brought together: rejection of the formal geometry and "academic rigidity" that characterized much of architecture, even of the irregular Gothic and Italianate houses, and looking to the colonial period for inspiration. The colonial had re-entered public awareness at the 1876 centennial, but most new houses looked elsewhere for inspiration. Now architects were turning to sources like the Fairbanks House to guide a less elaborate sense of design.

At first they were equally inspired by English country houses, which in turn

HISTORIC AMERICAN BUILDINGS SURVEY

Early houses like the 1636 Fairbanks House in Dedham, Massachusetts, (above) inspired architects like William Ralph Emerson to search for an architecture more suited to New England's traditions and landscapes, as in Emerson's 1896 Felsted in Deer Isle (facing page).

Henry Hobson Richardson's 1882 Stoughton House in Cambridge, Massachusetts, (above) established the style. Felsted (right and facing page) was one of its grandest achievements for the harmony of its lines and the aptness of its detailing.

looked to Tudor and Jacobean models. Many of them had clay tiling "hanging" in the exterior, but, as published in magazine engravings they appeared to American eyes to be covered in shingles. The American imitations were wood-framed and shingled, but were often just as historically inspired and complicated as their English models.

The work of two Boston architects changed that. The first was Henry Hobson Richardson, who devoted his short career primarily to large masonry buildings such as Trinity Church in Boston and the Marshall Field Department Store in Chicago; but he also designed some smaller shingled houses. His 1882 Stoughton House in Cambridge, Massachusetts, shows a freedom from historic motifs, but also great restraint and discipline in the use of a limited range of materials and forms.

The other was William Ralph Emerson, the son of a couple from Kennebunk. Largely self-taught in Boston, where some of the country's best architects were at work, Emerson applied his love of colonial architecture to the problem of summer houses, usually by the sea. According to Roger Reed, from his book *A Delight to All Who Know It,* the Boston Society of Architects said in a tribute to Emerson on his death in 1918:

> He was the creator of the shingle country house of the New England coast, and taught his generation how to use local materials without apology, but rather with pride in their rough and homespun character. He was keenly alive to the picturesque in nature and in art . . . . those who knew him in the earlier days of his activity . . . can justly estimate the great value of his influence in liberating architectural design from artificiality and in making simple and natural means artistically effective.

In Maine he designed many of the shingled cottages on Mount Desert Island, where Bar Harbor and Seal Harbor were becoming the rustic alternative to Newport, Rhode Island. His early house "Redwood," the 1879 Morrill cottage, owes a great deal to English precedents and to Henry Hobson Richardson's 1874 Watts Sherman house in Newport, But Emerson's later houses show increasingly fluid forms relating to the possibilities of the site. His house for Frederick Law Olmsted on Deer Isle is his masterpiece. "Felsted", built in 1890, sits on a high stone base at the water's edge. The house is bent to allow the wings to look out in slightly different directions. The ends of the main hipped roof extend down at each end, as if anchoring the house to the ground, while the central gable projects out over the sea. Ship's knees serve as brackets for the rough porch posts, and the windows are doublehung, with small panes in the upper sash and larger ones in the lower—the "cottage" windows that would become an emblem of the style.

Stevens and Cobb's 1888 book placed Maine in the forefront of architectural fashion with drawings like the one for Stevens' own house (top) and the iconic House by the Sea (above). Franklin Roosevelt's mother bought the family a summer house on Campobello Island, built in the Shingle Style in 1909.

Inside, the rooms are open to each other wherever possible, so the space seems to flow from room to room and outside to the sea and forest. The house does not pursue the ratification of stylishness, but rather the opportunities of the site's sea and sun. This type of house was the forerunner of the new century's modernist ethic of design determined not by precedent but by function and space.

Richardson and Emerson were pioneers, but they had many followers, not least of whom were two young architects in Portland: Albert Winslow Cobb, who worked for Emerson, and John Calvin Stevens, who had run Portland architect Francis Fassett's Boston office, in the same building as Emerson's office. In 1888 the two young men joined forces and designed numerous shingled houses, actively advocating for the style. That year they published a manifesto, modestly titled *Examples of American Domestic Architecture*. Full of the exalted rhetoric of the time, it heavily criticized most English architecture as:

> . . . that vast agglomeration of ornateness, imitated from everything vainglorious under the sun . . . tokens of the pride and materialism against which the voices of England's prophets are warning her. . . . In truth there is little to commend in any of the Renaissance architecture of continental Europe; architecture inspired by an admiration for tyrants for the work of their archetypes in the splendid, corrupt days of ancient Rome.

Instead, they praised the "excellent specimens" of design by Americans "groping after a…national style." These include Richardson and Emerson and their contemporaries. Cobb and Stevens also looked to "the examples, here in our own America, left us by the men who thought and fought out the Revolution…" And, in a burst of passion, they rejected the cult of novelty and called upon the need for rational design:

Being thus beset by examples of what has been built before it is vain to discuss the possibility of inventing "a new Architecture." To build rationally in an "original style" is no more possible than to furnish society with a useful code of "original statutes," in which shall appear no trace of the commands of Moses, or of the laws of Greece and Rome. Mark well the expression, "to build rationally." It is easy enough to build in a merely original fashion; we have most abundant and most lamentable evidence of that. But the rational, virtuous types—the worthy models in Architecture, prepared for us by past experience and best fitted to our present needs, are few; and are positive, graceful, orderly in their nature. Holding faithfully to these tried and proven types as bases of our modern design, we may nevertheless find plentiful opportunity for variety in the work based upon them.

Shingle Style interiors were much simpler than the Queen Anne, but they compensated by bringing in the outdoors, with wide and carefully placed windows.

Their book is full of their own small and simply detailed houses, along with sketches for summer cottages that were a growing phenomenon along the coast and lakes. With generally increased wealth, more people were able to imitate the rich, having a vacation home where the family spent the summer while the father commuted to work and returned for weekends. This pattern unintentionally replicated the migratory ways of Maine Indians, who spent the fall and winter inland and migrated to the coast in the summer to feast on fish and oysters—were we finally learning the lessons of civilization of our native predecessors?

Stevens and Cobb submitted the book to *American Architect and Building News,* challenging the magazine to "hit away at us in your review." The editor responded positively and the book became a national critical success, helping to spread the idea of simpler, more modest houses close to the land and suited to their neighborhoods—ideas we are still trying to learn.

There are two examples that stand out. One was the house Stevens designed for himself in Portland. It adopted the gambrel roof that Emerson loved to use, but simplified the house so that the one gambrel, broken only by small dormers and an inset balcony, covered the whole house and brought it

Campobello's bunkroom gives a good idea of the lightness and informality of these houses. In important ways they point toward the openness of modern design.

lower, radically departing from the towers and turrets that strove to make even a small house seem like a castle.

The other outstanding example was the drawing for the "House by the Sea," which was much larger but was held together by a great gable roof starting at the first floor and, again, sweeping the whole house into a single composition. By making the first-floor walls of stone, Stevens tried to eliminate the "wall" altogether, as if the roof sat on the foundation. With images like these, Stevens and Cobb helped turn America away from excess and toward a "irrational" balance of building with nature. These ideas informed architects throughout the country, and for the first—and arguably the last—time, Maine was in the vanguard of new thinking about architecture.

Even the functional "back rooms" are full of light.

Clusters of houses like these were built in the Portland area—Cushing Island and Delano Park still retain the flavor of their original character. Houses in the new suburbs of Portland were built for more than summer use; some were even built by sympathetic mill owners to serve as workers' housing.

There are still a great many of the original cottages to be discovered along the coast of Maine. They are sometimes so well integrated that they seem to disappear into the wooded terrain. For me, they are the greatest of Maine's houses, because they do not try to be great. They try to fit in.

One that has achieved a different kind of greatness through association is just across the Canadian border on Campobello Island. It is Franklin Delano Roosevelt's summer cottage, which the family referred to as "Campo." His mother bought the house in 1909 from its original owner, Mrs. Hartman Kuhn of Boston, who had a Boston architect, Willard Sears, and a Maine builder construct it in 1897. In 1915 Franklin oversaw an addition. The house is preserved of course for its Roosevelt connection, but it also gives us a chance to see a shingle cottage as it was lived in. The design uses the favored gambrel roof, and though the bright red-and-green exterior seems at odds with the desire to blend into nature, the shape of the house itself follows the site and avoids "agglomerations of ornateness" in the proper way.

The shingle style looked to two sources—fitting into nature and imitating the founding fathers—but as houses became more and more formally colonial, the second imperative gradually won out over the first. It was probably too much to expect that a century of following style leaders would so easily lead to new patterns of building. The idea of building with nature was taken over by Frank Lloyd Wright and the other "prairie" architects, as well as by Gustav Stickley with his Craftsman cottages and bungalows, but the prevailing style at the start of the 20th century was based on the 18th century and came to be called "colonial," as if the Revolution had been a mistake. 🐚

And of course the porches bring the indoors outside and toward the view to the sea. Pinecrest (left) in Camden, is a good example of the Shingle Style by local builder Cyrus Porter Brown.

CHRISTOPHER GLASS

COLONIAL REVIVAL

1876–Present

*M*ost of the architects who continued to work in the new century soon changed from the

free forms of the Shingle Style and accepted the discipline of the Federal style. Stevens himself used his initial success not to pursue new forms, but to refine his mastery of earlier models. Others would do the same.

On Mount Desert Island, Fred Savage designed and built a number of remarkable shingle cottages, such as Rosserne, of 1891, with its remarkable exterior stair that extends the upper plane of the gambrel roof nearly to the ground. On the same house Savage reworked the "candlesnuffer" corner tower with wraparound porch into an encompassing bower. As the new century dawned, he found his clients wanted stricter interpretations of period styles—generally colonial, but also the earlier Tudor style as well. Savage's own house, the Atlantean, built in 1903, adopted the newly strict Tudor, as did the large Breakwater cottage of the same year. The Breakwater shows the transition, because while it is Tudor on the outside, with rusticated stone and half-timbering, the interior is pure colonial, with white trim and classical columns. The stair hall is a fantasia on flying stairs from the Federal period, but it is not a new architectural style.

Stevens himself went the same way. In his book he had said "as well weary of the chaste elm tree as of the stately ionic column" and in his house designs he moved more and more toward a purer use of historic models. In 1900 he designed the Psi Upsilon Fraternity House at Bowdoin as a variation of the House by the Sea. By 1906, in the Webb House in Portland's West End, Stevens entirely followed the Georgian and Federal canon. His son and partner, John Howard, Stevens tried to justify this newly strict kind of design by saying it was "very satisfactory in its proportions and details, and yet not an historical copy of an old house, but a new creation of the same style, and with the same feeling that is evident in the best old colonial work."[3] He sounds more than a bit defensive, as if he secretly lamented his lost architectural freedom.

A stricter view of historical precedent informs the Colonial Revival, as in the remodeling of the Blaine House in Augusta (facing page) or the Tudor exterior and colonial interior of Fred Savage's Breakwater in Bar Harbor (above).

Stevens' Ionic sunroom center to the Blaine House of 1919 (top) is in sharp contrast to his Psi Upsilon house at Bowdoin of 1900 (above). The times changed, and Stevens changed with them.

In 1919 Stevens was called upon to remodel the Blaine House to serve as the governor's residence in Augusta. The house had started as a simple Federal block in 1833, acquired a Greek Revival front porch, and, after its 1862 purchase by James G. Blaine, was given an Italianate wing in 1872 containing a separate office and billiard room. Stevens tied the two wings together with a conservatory, supported by four prominent ionic columns. Thus, the house came full circle to its origins, while retaining fragmented evidence of its other incarnations. As such, it is perhaps a fitting symbol of the government it represents—always trying new ways of organization yet constantly being recalled to its roots.

Such great houses as there were in Maine tended to be classical. Near the capitol Stevens designed the Governor Hill House, an exercise in the giant order of imperial Rome. It served for a while as a Catholic retreat, and seemed right at home. Stevens's grandest exercise in the colonial estate was Elmhurst, the 1913 house for John Sedgwick Hyde, president of Bath Iron Works. Grand parlors, sweeping formal gardens, even a Roman-themed indoor swimming pool, make Elmhurst Maine's equivalent of William Randolph Hearst's La Cuesta

Stevens' sparlors and sunroom were pure Colonial Revival, light and white.

Encantada at San Simeon. The interior decoration was even done by Addison Mizner (of Mediterranean Revival fame) before he moved to Florida and built Palm Beach. The barn and "farmer's cottage," however, recall the now abandoned soft rooflines of the shingle style, embalmed now with stucco walls. The house today is the home of the Hyde School and this use is much more compatible with the size of the house than a single-family residence was.

A grand house along the same lines and following the plans of Boston architect Guy Lowell was built in York in 1905. Called River House, it was the summer home of the B. F. Goodrich family. In 1927 an employee burned it to disguise a burglary and the house was rebuilt by Portland architect Herbert Rhodes, who included a few Mediterranean accents popular at the time. The beautifully landscaped grounds were done by Arthur Shurcliff, who was the landscape architect for the restoration of Colonial Williamsburg. River

Compare this Portland house (facing page) with the Lady Pepperrell (p.24). The 20th century saw the rebirth of grand country houses modeled on those of the 18th century, such as River House in York, designed originally by Guy Lowell in 1905.

GREG CURRIER

House represents the high-water mark of the Colonial Revival country house—restrained in its architecture, generous in its landscape, elegant in its details. In 1974 it was given to Bowdoin College with a life tenancy for the last heir, Mary Marvin Breckinridge Patterson. At the time of her death in 2004, Bowdoin decided it couldn't afford to keep the house as the conference and educational center it had been, and it was sold to new owners. Fortunately, the new owners have kept the house as it was and even opened it to the public for the first time for an event sponsored by Old York Historical Society's centennial celebration of the house's construction.

This is a reminder of one of the best aspects of the Colonial Revival. It was largely due to the spirit of the Colonial Revival that historical societies sprang up throughout the state, often centered on protecting a local landmark threatened with destruction. The 1920s are remembered as the Jazz Age, but they were even more the age of patriotic enthusiasm for the founders, especially in the years around the sesquicentennial in 1926. If the 1876 centennial had planted the seed, by 1926 it was in full flower. Longfellow House had led the way, becoming a museum in 1901, and 1929 was the year the DAR achieved the rebuilding of Montpelier, with the help of the sympathetic publisher of the *Ladies' Home Journal* and the *Saturday Evening Post*. The lush landscapes of Maxfield Parrish, punctuated with white colonial farmhouses and classical maidens, were on every calendar, creating an idyllic vision of New England. It is to this cultural phenomenon that we owe the continued existence of many of Maine's great houses, and we should be profoundly grateful. 🧠

River House (above and facing page) is surrounded by formal gardens designed by Arthur Shurcliff. The Colonial Revival (right) remains a popular style and houses of its type are quite common.

GREG CURRIER

MODERNISM

1936–Present

$\mathcal{M}$odern architecture has never been truly accepted in Maine. Modernism is the

rejection of history in favor of innovation, and Maine has never been a state to ignore its past and has always been wary of innovation. There have been examples of modern houses here and there, and of architects trying repeat-edly to convince a skeptical public of the benefits of glass and steel over shingles and logs, but Maine remains stubbornly wedded to its farmhouses and villages and shingled cottages.

Harvard's School of Design became the cen-ter of orthodox modernism in America after Walter Gropius, founder of the Bauhaus School in Germany, came here fleeing the Nazis and was appointed head of the school. Some Bauhaus architects associated with Harvard, particularly Marcel Breuer, designed houses in Maine. The earliest modern house, though, was Fortune Rocks, designed in 1936 for Clara Fargo Thomas at the head of Somes Sound on Mount Des-ert Island. In this house Philadelphia architect George Howe—who had gone from designing classical coun-try houses on the Main Line to working with William Lescaze on America's first modern skyscraper, the PFSF bank building in Phil-adelphia—created an almost Japanese pavilion cantilevered over the bay on huge concrete beams.

MHPC

The principal monument to modern-ism in Maine is the Anchorage (facing page), Nelson Rockefeller's summer house in Seal Harbor, designed in 1941 by Wallace K. Harrison. Fortune Rocks (above) was the first Modernist house in the state.

But the crowning achievement of the first generation of modernists was the Anchorage, a sweeping house designed in 1941 for Nelson Rockefeller by Wallace K. Harrison. Harrison is best known as the chief architect of the United Nations complex, and he brought a sense of formal innovation to the Anchorage project. The site is a rugged peninsula, with coves and promon-tories on the sides. The house is a vast curve, designed so rooms and decks command as many of these different landscape features as possible before

Each room of the Anchorage (top and facing page) faces a different view of the sea as the house curves to follow the site. The center of the house is a curving stair inside a lighthouse–shaped tower. This Modernist house in Lewiston (above) shows the influence of Frank Lloyd Wright's Usonian Style.

tailing off in a straight staff wing. The dramatic centerpiece is a lighthouse-shaped tower, within which a flying spiral stair diminishes in diameter as it rises though the cone-shaped interior. After Rockefeller's death, the family sold the house to the Ford family, which continues to cope with its maintenance. It would be nice to think that as "Campo" has become a public building—and perhaps one day the Bush house at Walker's Point might be—so the home of a vice president might be a candidate for a "historic modern" house museum. The spectacular site, however, like that of Walker's Point, probably ensures that the house will remain private for years to come.

Another much smaller modernist monument is the live-in laboratory called Orgonon, built in 1947 by Wilhelm Reich in the Rangeley region. Technically more than a house, it is in form one of the nearest things to a Bauhaus-inspired house in Maine, certainly among buildings open to the public. All right angles and flat roofs, clustered picturesquely on its hilltop site, it evokes the houses of Gropius and Richard Neutra. The house is a shrine to its owner's quest for a unifying theory of physics based on his discovery of "orgone" energy, and it is a testament to the modernist spirit, alive on a hilltop in the Maine mountains.

The Anchorage's stair gets smaller as it rises (facing page). The house takes advantage of its dramatic site (above). Orgonon, (left) a house with similar but much more modest features, crowns a hilltop above Rangeley.

THE LAST FEW YEARS

It is premature to decide what houses of the last decades will be considered "great." Recent houses have not acquired historic status or been made into house museums—yet. The rules of the National Register of Historic Places specify that no building less than fifty years of age can be designated "historic," and that is probably a good limit. It takes a couple of generations for us to come to a consensus about what has lasting value.

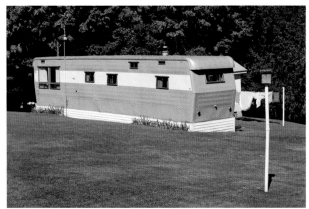

CHRISTOPHER GLASS

Mobile homes started by imitating railroad cars. Today they look like houses, usually Colonial Revival in style.

We have seen broad but gradual changes in house building over the last half century, as the persistent preference for the colonial has jockeyed with new forces. In the postwar years, mobile homes made their appearance, at first based on the vehicles their designers chose to emulate—airplanes and passenger trains. As it became clear that their one "mobile" trip was from factory to site, however, the mobile homes began to evolve into imitations of stick-built houses, and today most are some variation on the colonial style. Today, manufactured and prefabricated houses are a very large part of the housing stock, but they are not very different architecturally from other houses, which mostly tend toward colonial, but with still some hints of shingle or even Queen Anne style.

The energy crisis of the 1970s caused or at least coincided with an attempt to redefine house building in terms of scientific and engineering problems in energy conservation, as exemplified by the work of the Shelter Institute in Woolwich. Passive-solar houses capable of storing heat energy were designed and built, often by owners who had studied the techniques at the school. With luck, these will come to be considered the prescient forerunners of more environmentally responsible houses of the future, but as the energy crisis abated, the enthusiasm for these houses waned, and Maine returned to tradition.

There have also been a few modernist housing developments—especially in places like the ski resort area around Sugarloaf—of shed-roofed modern houses with vertical siding that grew out of the modernist developments in the suburbs of Boston and the Bay region of California. In 1960 Edward Larabee Barnes designed the Haystack School in Deer Isle and a number of similar houses along the coast. Later, younger architects such as Peter Forbes of Boston designed elegant modernist houses on Mount Desert Island and Deer Isle.

Maine saw a new flowering of shingled cottages in the 1980s as a generation exposed to Vincent Scully's writings on the Shingle Style came to maturity. Excellent examples of modest, simply detailed cottages thoughtfully connected to their landscapes were built throughout the state. Robert A. M. Stern—who had studied at Yale with Scully, and with Robert Venturi and Charles Moore,

A new generation of houses based on traditional models fits the landscape and the history of the state.

both advocates of a softer and more historically informed approach to modern architecture—built a series of houses that started out looking like those of his teachers, but gradually evolved into an unapologetic embrace of the Colonial Revival qualities of the Shingle Style, much as John Calvin Stevens had a century earlier. Stern's houses became the principal prototype for a great many of the new houses of the last years.

Various economic bubbles have had their way with house-building. Sizes and costs have ballooned in Maine as elsewhere, and inflated values have priced "natives" out of the market, in many cases compelling them to sell newly valuable—and therefore heavily taxed—houses and move to less attractive areas.

The severe recession of 2009 may mark a new era of forced restraint in house building. Though it will involve real pain for many, in the medium and long run the results could have beneficial effects. Artificially inflated land values may moderate, and artificially inflated houses may lose popularity, as the Queen Anne extravagances did in the 1890s. New ways of saving and generating energy may finally fulfill the promise of the Shelter Institute's dreams. New patterns of development, less dependent on the car and the single house, may emerge. Reinvigorated village life may restore community without its traditional insularity.

This older remodeled house by the architecture firm, Elliott Elliott and Norelius shows the exterior discipline (above) and interior imagination (facing page) that make for a great Maine house.

Out of the downfall of the Queen Anne came the high point of our long and complex story—the modest yet imaginative cottage of the early Shingle era. Maybe, with imagination and discipline, we can rediscover what Stevens and Cobb called "the rational, virtuous types—the worthy models in Architecture, prepared for us by past experience and best fitted to our present needs."

I hope, as we build the future, that we honor and respect the past. Each generation builds what it thinks is best at the time, and from each generation we are fortunate to have at least some survivors, zealously defended by a citizen militia called preservationists. Even if to our eyes some of these look like monuments to folly, folly is worth remembering, if only to avoid repeating it.

LIVING IN HISTORIC HOUSES

Of course, not all old houses can become house museums. Most still serve as homes. While the systems and weathertightness of old houses certainly need updating, it is important that the architectural values of their builders not be sacrificed. By buying an old house, we assume its history and join the procession of those who have lived there before. We are not its masters, we are its stewards in our generation. We are responsible for the changes made, for the maintenance done or deferred, for the way our house participates in the

conversation of its neighborhood. Fortunately, these days, there is a greater appreciation for houses built in other times, with materials and methods other than what are commonly used. Many of the ìquick fixes,î such as vinyl siding and replacement windows, have been shown to do lasting damage without doing more than simply deferring the problems they promise to solve forever.

It is undoubtedly true, though, that owning a historic house requires more thought and more work than living in a more recently built one. It is often a matter of trying to understand how the house wants you to live. Once, on a panel about energy use, I said the best way to be comfortable in an old house was to wear a sweater. The builders of these houses knew what was expected of them—they closed off rooms in the winter and paid attention in the design to how to live according to the seasons. They kept after the maintenance and made sure to catch any breaches before serious damage was done. All of this makes common sense, but we aren't used to living this way.

And many of these houses were built in the age of large families, and the age of live-in servants. Houses that are too large for our times can often be adapted to new and creative uses. Many, like Norumbega, have been converted to bed and breakfasts, others to offices and schools, such as Elmhurst. Those who see the possibilities in these memorials to our predecessors' ambitions are to be honored for finding ways to keep them alive into the next generation.

While we should not feel that we cannot make changes needed to adapt our houses to new needs, we should also learn to appreciate the values the house embodies. Learning the stories of the owners, or of the styles and builders of our architectural history, is a way of coming to know more profoundly what it means to call a place "home." It is a form of what T.S. Eliot meant when he wrote:

> We shall not cease from exploration
> And the end of all our exploring
> Will be to arrive where we started
> And know the place for the first time.

Old houses continue their role of recalling the past and adapting to the present, as in this Cape in Days Ferry.

We do not truly know where we live until we know its history, and the dreams of those who have lived here before we came along.

What we have seen is that those dreams themselves involved history. Our earliest real architecture, the Georgian style, consisted of looking through

English eyes at Italian versions of ancient Roman originals. Through the 19th century we chose one style after another based on the cultural significance of foreign approaches to building—the Greek, the Gothic, the Italianate, the Second Empire—and each of those styles was based on celebrating the principles of a previous historic period. Finally, through the excesses of the Queen Anne and the simplicities of the Shingle Style, we settled on a Colonial Revival intended to reinstate the virtues of our founding fathers. Modernists tried to abolish history altogether, in favor of the supposed purity of the machine, but there were few adherents. More recently the Shingle Style has reappeared, while a new generation of modernists has tried to reintroduce the—by now historical—modernist style. Everything we have built, everything we can build, involves making decisions about what we value in our architectural history. We can let others make those decisions for us, or we can think about what our values are and make sure that what we build reflects those values.

Vincent Scully once wrote about the architecture of Louis Kahn, stating that Kahn's buildings projected an image of wholeness, matched only by those of Wright and Le Corbusier. "Such rarity," Scully said, "should not be considered surprising, as it is linked to that rarest of human gifts, the instinct for how and what to remember."[4]

Old houses find new uses. This attic in the Hartley Lord house has become a rustic study (below), while the Italianate-updated Federal house in Camden (left) has become a bed and breakfast.

Map of Historic Maine Homes

These are some of the historic houses open as house museums, but there are a significant number of local historical societies with small museums, many in houses. Houses mentioned in the book, but not open to the public, are not shown to protect the privacy of the owners.

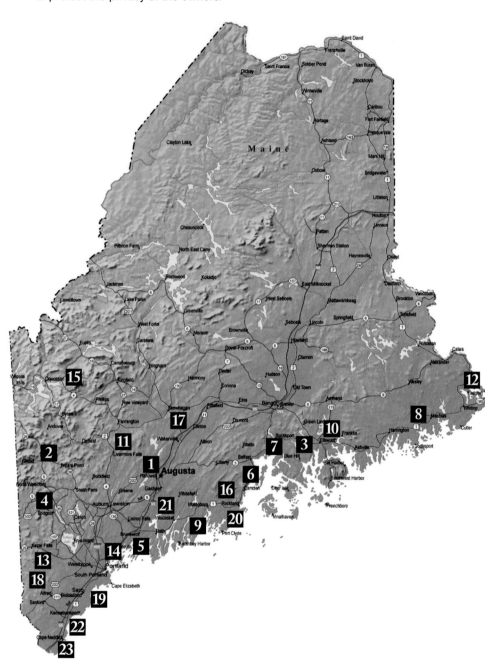

The Maine State House can be seen over the roof of the Blaine House.

1. **Augusta**
   Blaine House

2. **Bethel**
   Dr. Moses Mason House

3. **Blue Hill**
   Hendricks Hill Museum

4. **Bridgton**
   Rufus Porter Museum

5. **Brunswick**
   Joshua Lawrence Chamberlain Museum
   Skolfield-Whittier House/Pejepscot Museum

6. **Camden**
   The Conway Homestead

7. **Castine**
   Wilson Museum (John Perkins House)

8. **Columbia Falls**
   Ruggles House

9. **Damariscotta**
   Chapman-Hall House

10. **Ellsworth**
    The Black House/Woodlawn Museum

11. **Livermore**
    Washburn-Norlands Living History Center

12. **Lubec**
    Campobello

13. **Newfield**
    Willowbrook Village

14. **Portland**
    McClellan-Sweat House
    Tate House
    Victoria Mansion
    Wadsworth-Longfellow House

15. **Rangeley**
    Orgonon

16. **Rockland**
    Farnsworth Art Museum
    (Olson House, Cushing)

17. **Skowhegan**
    History House

18. **South Berwick**
    Hamilton House

19. **Southport**
    Hendricks Hill

20. **Thomaston**
    Monpelier (Knox Mansion)

21. **Wiscasset**
    Castle Tucker
    Nickels-Sortwell House

22. **York**
    Museums of Old York

23. **York Harbor**
    Sayward-Wheeler House

NOTES

1 Deborah Thompson, ed.: *Maine Forms of American Architecture,* Waterville ME.: Colby College, 1976, p. 28

2 Quoted in a speech by by Alexander Karanikas, Professor of English Emeritus University of Illinois at Chicago, at *www.helleniccomserve. com/karanikasindependencespeech.html*

3 John Calvin Stevens II and Earle G. Shettleworth, Jr., *John Calvin Stevens: Domestic Architecture 1930-1930*, Scarborough, Maine, Harp Publications, 1990, p. 196.

4 Vincent Scully, *Louis I Kahn,* New York, George Braziller, 1962. P?

Let us hope that these reminders of our history continue their presence among us. We need the example of places like Colonel Black's house to set the standard for our own additions to the number of Maine's historic houses.

Acknowledgments

Brian Vanden Brink has had the opportunity to photograph many of Maine's most important houses and many of those pictures accompanied articles in *Down East* magazine over the last twenty years, many of them written by Ellen MacDonald Ward. Those houses are the core of the book. Other sources have played a major role in my understanding of this story. Chief among them is the work of the Maine Historic Preservation Commission, which administers the National Register of Historic Places for Maine and works tirelessly to identify and protect our historic buildings and landscapes. I have had the pleasure and privilege of serving on the Commission and, working with the private organization Maine Preservation, of helping to promote and protect the work of the Commission and to extend its reach. The two groups' numerous publications and lectures and conferences educate the people of Maine about the importance of understanding why it is necessary to keep these reminders of our past in our present, and the programs they administer provide both technical help and some financial assistance—though never enough—to those charged with that task around the state. An early Commission publication was Frank Beard's booklet *200 Years of Maine Housing,* which is the direct antecedent of this work.

Another influence that set me on this path was the exhibit and book *Maine Forms of American Architecture,* sponsored by Colby College Museum of Art and published by Down East Books to celebrate the nation's bicentennial in 1976. Deborah Thompson of Bangor brought together experts on the different eras and produced an impressive collections of essays on various aspects of Maine's architectural history.

Many other sources were consulted in writing this book. Today most historic house museums have good web sites, and there are not a few books on specific aspects of this history. One invaluable source is the out-of-print *Maine Catalog* by Denys Peter Myers, which links the buildings listed in the National Register in a historic narrative. Others are mentioned in the text that follows. The Historic American Buildings Survey (HABS), begun as a Depression-relief project in the 1930s, has execellent plans and photographs of many of the houses, available on its web site.

And Elizabeth Bouvé has supplied some of the photographs that Brian didn't have. She attended one of my lectures and volunteered to improve the old images I was using by taking new photographs of many of the houses.

My thanks go to Michael Steere, who skillfully polished the rough edges off my story while leaving its shape intact, and to my good friend Earle Shettleworth, for reviewing the text and catching a lot of the historical errors my less-disciplined scholarship is prone to. Any that he missed are, of course, my fault.

A view of the marvelous lunette window in Wiscasset's Nickels–Sortwell House.

A Summary of Styles

 **COLONIAL** *1600-1720* Maine's first buildings were based on rural English models and were gradually adapted to Maine's climate and materials. Most surviving houses are either garrisons solidly built of squared and stacked logs protected by clapboard or shingle siding or capes, simple rectangles with center chimneys and steep roofs with joined timber frames. These often acquired ells and sheds to become connected farm buildings. Windows were small, with small glass panes.

 **GEORGIAN** *1720-1780* As wealth increased, houses adopted the English preference for classical Roman design based on the work of Italian architect Andrea Palladio. Houses grew larger, and classical details around doorways and cornices became common. Chimneys moved from the center to make room for grand stairways. Larger-paned windows were set in carefully proportioned symmetrical facades.

 **FEDERAL** *1780-1830* After the Revolution, houses continued to be based on English models. Classical detail became more delicate, and there was a greater variety of elements; still there was no dramatic change from the formality of the Georgian style.

 **GREEK REVIVAL** *1820-1850* As the Greek people rebelled against Turkish rule, and as archaeological expeditions published drawings of ancient Greek architecture, an interest in buildings in the style of ancient Greece swept Europe and America. Houses suddenly had their gable ends turned to the street and treated as temple fronts, with full height, free-standing columns or attached pilasters and tall windows. Heavy cornices with plain detailing replaced the intricate ornaments of the previous age. It was a revolutionary architecture at last.

 **GOTHIC REVIVAL** *1840-1860* The popularity of literary works set in the middle ages, along with the advocacy of Andrew Jackson Downing for a more virtuous way of building brought about Gothic design. Stone—or vertical boards and batten if stone was unavailable or too expensive— became the ideal. House plans and rooflines were irregular to "honestly" express the different spaces, and a profusion of ornamentation was based on the carved stonework of the days before the classical revivals. Bay windows and porches connected the inside to the outside in new ways.

ITALIANATE *1850–1880* A German preference for the architecture of northern Italy spread to England with Queen Victoria's marriage to German Prince Albert. The style combined round arches and classical detail with the irregular plans of Italian farms. Roofs were low-pitched with wide overhangs supported by elaborate brackets. Often a tall, square tower dominated the roofline and a cupola created a central light well. Rooms had high ceilings and tall windows that opened to piazzas and terraces.

SECOND EMPIRE *1860–1880* After Albert's death and with the renewal of Paris under Napoleon III, the French style of steep roofs punctuated by tall dormers became the fashion. Called the Mansard roof after a 17th-century architect, it was a variation on the Italianate style.

QUEEN ANNE *1880–1900* Mysteriously named for the 18th-century English queen, this style was an amalgam of elements from all the previous styles. Wildly irregular plans, with towers, dormers, and porches produced the most elaborate houses ever seen. Machine-made ornaments were heavily used and promoted by mail-order catalogs and plan books. Variants included the Stick Style and the German baronial castles.

SHINGLE STYLE *1890–1910* A reaction to the excesses of the Queen Anne, this style sought to recapture the simplicity and naturalness of early New England building. Wood shingles were the exterior material of choice, and rooflines merged to make the house seem to grow out of the surrounding natural landscape. Windows and porches were placed to take advantage of views and weather. Simple detailing, in part based on Japanese design, rejected the ornamental riot of the Queen Anne. The style was mostly used for vacation cottages and rural retreats.

COLONIAL REVIVAL *1876–Present* This style was a reaction to the European fashions that followed one after the other and became more and more elaborate. Essentially, it sought to recreate the architecture of the 18th century and earlier. By the early 1900s it was the accepted style, and remained the official American style through much of the 20th century, especially around the 1926 sesquicentennial. Even today capes and symmetrical two-story "colonials" make up much of new house building.

MODERNISM *1936– Present* This is the European movement to reject historical associations in favor of a design based on the aesthetic of the machine. Form should follow function, not fashion. Flat roofs, plate-glass windows, rigorously asymmetrical plans, open flow between rooms, and the complete absence of ornamentation were required. Except for its milder form in houses based on Frank Lloyd Wright's work and California's Ranch houses, the style has never been more than an occasional experiment. More recently the Shingle Style has made a comeback in Postmodernism, which has been more popular.

INDEX